What Do Great Teachers Say?

Do you remember a time when you used the right words at the right moment, and they made all the difference? With the aim of helping you repeat that experience every day, this book provides hundreds of examples of what we call Great Teacher Language, a technique designed to help all teachers use words to transform student behavior and parent relationships. In their years of working at the K-12 levels, educators Hal Holloman and Peggy H. Yates have identified the exact phrases and key words you can use in your classroom to address inappropriate outbursts, a lack of respect and cooperation, student conflict, and more. Great Teacher Language will enable you to transform student behavior, parent relationships, and your classroom culture.

This book features 11 Great Teacher Language Word Categories, which you'll learn how to use in terms of self-talk, student talk, and parent talk: Words of Accountability, Words of Encouragement, Words of Grace, Words of Guidance, Words of High Expectations, Words of Hope, Words of Love, Words of Relationships, Words of Respect, Words of Understanding, and Words of Unity.

Filled with helpful charts and Great Teacher Language examples, this resource will be one you turn to again and again and will make a transformational difference for your students, your parents, and you!

Hal Holloman has experience as a teacher, coach, assistant principal, and principal at various levels. Currently, he is a Professor of Educational Leadership at East Carolina University and Director of the ECU Pirate Leadership Academy, where he teaches in the Masters of School Administration program and coaches new school leaders.

Peggy H. Yates has over 35 years of experience in the field of education, including positions as an elementary and middle school teacher, district-level K-8 curriculum and instruction director, higher education administrator, and Associate Professor in the College of Education at East Carolina University.

Also Available from Routledge Eye On Education
(www.routledge.com/k-12)

What Do Great Teachers Say? Language All Teachers Can Use to Transform Student Behavior, Parent Relationships, and Classroom Culture, 6-12
Hal Holloman and Peggy H. Yates

Classroom Management from the Ground Up
Todd Whitaker, Katherine Whitaker, Madeline Whitaker Good

Your First Year, 2e: How to Survive and Thrive as a New Teacher
Todd Whitaker, Katherine Whitaker, Madeline Whitaker Good

The Student Motivation Handbook: 50 Ways to Boost an Intrinsic Desire to Learn
Larry Ferlazzo

75 Quick and Easy Solutions to Common Classroom Disruptions
Bryan Harris and Cassandra Harris

What Do Great Teachers Say?

Language All Teachers Can Use to Transform Student Behavior, Parent Relationships, and Classroom Culture K-5

Hal Holloman and Peggy H. Yates

Routledge
Taylor & Francis Group
NEW YORK AND LONDON

First published 2024
by Routledge
605 Third Avenue, New York, NY 10158

and by Routledge
4 Park Square, Milton Park, Abingdon, Oxon, OX14 4RN

Routledge is an imprint of the Taylor & Francis Group, an informa business

© 2024 Hal Holloman and Peggy H. Yates

The right of Hal Holloman and Peggy H. Yates to be identified as authors of this work has been asserted in accordance with sections 77 and 78 of the Copyright, Designs and Patents Act 1988.

All rights reserved. No part of this book may be reprinted or reproduced or utilised in any form or by any electronic, mechanical, or other means, now known or hereafter invented, including photocopying and recording, or in any information storage or retrieval system, without permission in writing from the publishers.

Trademark notice: Product or corporate names may be trademarks or registered trademarks, and are used only for identification and explanation without intent to infringe.

Concepts from this book were previously published as *What Do You Say When…? Best Practice Language for Improving Student Behavior* by Hal Holloman and Peggy H. Yates, Copyright © March 2010.

Library of Congress Cataloging-in-Publication Data
Names: Yates, Peggy H., author. | Holloman, Hal, author.
Title: What do great teachers say? : Language all teachers can use to transform student behavior, parent relationships, and classroom culture K-5 / Peggy Yates and Hal Holloman
Description: New York : Routledge, 2024. | Series: Eye on education | Includes bibliographical references and index. |
Identifiers: LCCN 2023035800 (print) | LCCN 2023035801 (ebook) | ISBN 9781032508832 (hbk) | ISBN 9781032505855 (pbk) | ISBN 9781003400141 (ebk)
Subjects: LCSH: Classroom management. | Problem children--Behavior modification. | Parent-teacher relationships. | Communication in education.
Classification: LCC LB3013 .Y38 2024 (print) | LCC LB3013 (ebook) | DDC 371.102/4--dc23/eng/20230925
LC record available at https://lccn.loc.gov/2023035800
LC ebook record available at https://lccn.loc.gov/2023035801

ISBN: 978-1-032-50883-2 (hbk)
ISBN: 978-1-032-50585-5 (pbk)
ISBN: 978-1-003-40014-1 (ebk)

DOI: 10.4324/9781003400141

Typeset in Palatino
by SPi Technologies India Pvt Ltd (Straive)

Dedication

To our Heavenly Father—your love, grace, hope, and guidance are amazing!

To my beautiful wife, Blair—you are my soulmate and best friend. I love you!
—Hal Holloman

I dedicate this book to

All Teachers Everywhere
You touch students' hearts and minds every day. You make a difference in our world!

My Husband
You support me and love me unconditionally. You are my best friend!

My Children
You made us a family. You are my joy and happiness!

My Grandchildren
You make my heart smile and call me Nana. You are my grand love!

My Heavenly Father
My Rock and My Salvation
—Peggy Yates

Contents

List of Tables xi
Meet the Authors xii

Introduction 1

1 **Great Teacher Language: The Right Words at the Right Time** 4

2 **The 11 Great Teacher Language Word Categories and Frameworks for Transforming Student Behavior and Parent Relationships in the Classroom and Beyond** 8

3 **What Do Great Teachers Say on the First Day of School and the Days that Follow?** 31
    Standard 3.1: Setting High Expectations for All 33
    Standard 3.2: Establishing the Rules and Behavior Expectations for Success 36
    Standard 3.3: Creating a Culture of Community and Teamwork 39
    Standard 3.4: Encouraging Self-Management 42
    Standard 3.5: Leading by Example 45
    Standard 3.6: Building Relationships with Students and Their Families 48

4 **What Do Great Teachers Say When a Student Is Passively Disengaged?** 57
    Scenario 4.1: A Student is Texting on His Cell Phone or Scrolling through His Computer 60
    Scenario 4.2: A Student is Sleeping in Class 63
    Scenario 4.3: A Student is Not Working On His Assignment and Looks Embarrassed, Troubled, Stressed, And/Or Frustrated ... 65

Scenario 4.4: A Student is Not Paying Attention to the Lesson and is Daydreaming in Class.......66
Scenario 4.5: A Student Never Verbally Participates in Class...............................67
Scenario 4.6: A Passively Disengaged Student Has Failing Grades in Your Class.............69

5 What Do Great Teachers Say When a Student is an Attention Seeker?.....................................75

Scenario 5.1: A Student is Constantly Raising His/Her Hand and Saying, "Teacher, Teacher…"............................78
Scenario 5.2: A Student is Up Out of His/Her Seat… Socializing with Other Students, Throwing Away Trash, Sharpening His/Her Pencil, Etc. 79
Scenario 5.3: A Student Says, "Teacher, He's Bothering Me!"........................81
Scenario 5.4: A Student is Being the Class Entertainer....83
Scenario 5.5: A Student is Always Raising His/Her Hand Wanting to Answer Every Question or is Constantly Asking Questions................................85
Scenario 5.6: A Student is Always Talking in Class......87

6 What Do Great Teachers Say When a Student Outburst Happens?...91

Scenario 6.1: A Student Yells Out, "This is So Boring!"...93
Scenario 6.2: A Student Yells Out, "This is Stupid. I Can't Do It!"..........................94
Scenario 6.3: A Student Yells Out, "Why Do We Need To Learn This…?" 95
Scenario 6.4: A Student Yells Out Profanity, "@#$%".....97
Scenario 6.5: A Student Yells Out a Verbally Aggressive Outburst, and/or Acts Out a Physically Aggressive Outburst. 99

7 What Do Great Teachers Say When a Student Does Not Show Respect for Themselves or Others? 105

Scenario 7.1: A Student is Calling Other Students Names And/Or Making Fun of Other Students. 108

Scenario 7.2: A Student is Making Inappropriate Gestures At Other Students And/Or The Teacher. 111

Scenario 7.3: A Student is Verbally Disrespectful to the Teacher. 114

Scenario 7.4: A Student is Interrupting Another Student And/Or the Teacher. 117

Scenario 7.5: A Student is Taking Things That Do Not Belong to Him/Her. 118

Scenario 7.6: A Student is Demonstrating a Lack of Self-Respect. 121

8 What Do Great Teachers Say When a Student Refuses to Cooperate or Challenges Them? 126

Scenario 8.1: A Student Consistently Asks Questions That Challenge You And/Or the Lesson You Are Teaching. 131

Scenario 8.2: A Student Says, "I Don't Agree With You, Or I Don't Believe You, Or You Are Wrong!" 133

Scenario 8.3: A Student Refuses to Cooperate with You and Says, "You're Not My Mom... You Can't Tell Me What to Do! You Can't Make Me Do This Work!" 135

Scenario 8.4: A Student is Outwardly Angry and Blatantly Disrespectful Toward You. 140

9 What Do Great Teachers Say When a Student Conflict Occurs? 148

Scenario 9.1: Two Students are in a Small Disagreement and Are Not Getting Along With One Another. 153

Scenario 9.2:	Two Students Are Arguing With One Another................................155
Scenario 9.3:	A Student Pushes And/Or Shoves Another Student......................159
Scenario 9.4:	A Student Hits Another Student..........161
Scenario 9.5:	A Student is Bullying And/Or Cyberbullying Another Student..........166
Scenario 9.6:	Two Students Are Physically Fighting......172
Scenario 9.7:	A Student Hits the Teacher................177

10 Transforming your Classroom Culture into a Great Classroom Culture 184

Index of GTL Student Behavior Scenarios 197

Tables

2.1	The Great Teacher Language Framework for Transforming Student Behavior in the Classroom and Beyond	25
2.2	The Great Teacher Language Framework for Transforming Parent Relationships	28
10.1	The Great Classroom Culture Framework	185

Meet the Authors

Hal Holloman has experience in elementary, middle, and high schools as a teacher, coach, assistant principal, and principal. He grew up in rural eastern North Carolina in Aulander, NC and graduated from Bertie High School. He earned his BA in English from Wake Forest University, his Master of Arts in Educational Administration from East Carolina University, and his PhD in Educational Administration from the University of South Carolina.

Currently, he is a Professor of Educational Leadership at East Carolina University and Director of the ECU Pirate Leadership Academy, where he teaches in the Masters of School Administration program and coaches new school leaders in eastern North Carolina. His current research focuses on uncovering great educator language to coach and promote vitality and prevent burnout for school leaders, teachers, students, and parents. Dr. Holloman is coauthor of the book, *What Do You Say When...? Best Practice Language for Improving Student Behavior* and his works have been published in journals such as the *International Journal of Leadership Preparation, Journal of Positive Behavior Interventions, International Journal of Leadership in Education, School Leadership Review,* and the *Journal of Cases in Educational Leadership*.

He lives in Greenville, North Carolina with his wife, Blair, and they have four children: Luke, Zeke, Jessie, and Maggie.

Peggy H. Yates has over 35 years of experience in the field of education, including positions as an elementary and middle school teacher, district-level K-8 curriculum and instruction director, higher education administrator, and Associate Professor in the College of Education at East Carolina University. While at ECU, she taught elementary education methods courses in classroom management and curriculum. She earned a Bachelor of Arts in Elementary Education from Fairmont State College, a Master of Education from Tarleton State University, and a PhD in Organizational Leadership in Education from Regent University. Dr. Yates is coauthor of the book, *What Do You Say When…? Best Practice Language for Improving Student Behavior* and has written journal articles highlighting effective teaching strategies, classroom management, and Best Practice Language. She is now retired and lives in North Carolina with her husband, Merle. She has two children, Stephanie and Adam; and nine grandchildren, Hailey, Cole, Lorelei, Maddie, Annabelle, Emmyrose, David, Brandon, and Austin.

Introduction

This book is about great language all teachers can use every day to make a difference with students and parents. We call this great language—Great Teacher Language (GTL)! From our personal teaching experiences, when student behavior disruptions occurred or when parents were disconnected from school, we would ask ourselves, "What could I say right now to make a difference with this student or this parent?" Throughout this book, you'll find hundreds of GTL examples all teachers can use to transform student behavior, parent relationships, and your classroom culture.

The book is divided into ten chapters. Chapters 1 and 2 define and describe GTL and the GTL Frameworks for Transforming Student Behavior and Parent Relationships. Each framework consists of the 11 GTL Word Categories—Words of Accountability, Words of Encouragement, Words of Grace, Words of Guidance, Words of High Expectations, Words of Hope, Words of Love, Words of Relationships, Words of Respect, Words of Understanding, and Words of Unity—and provides teachers with a reflective model for turning their Language of Practice into GTL.

Chapter 3 strategically focuses on GTL you can use on the first day of school with students and parents. Chapters 4 through 9 present challenging classroom behavior scenarios. Each chapter begins with the question 'What Do Great Teachers Say?' and identifies four to seven specific student behavior scenarios that are common in today's classrooms. In each chapter, you'll also find relevant and helpful background information related to each classroom behavior scenario. All of these chapters offer teacher-friendly charts with *GTL Reminders to Self, GTL to Share with Students*, *GTL to Use When Talking and Communicating with Parents*, and *GTL Classroom Activities*.

- *GTL Reminders to Self* can be used by teachers to pause and reflect on what is happening with students and parents and why it might be happening. These GTL Reminders to Self are great self-coaching reminders to consider before speaking to students and parents.
- *GTL to Share with Students* provide teachers with GTL to use before, during, or after student behavior scenarios occur. These GTL examples can be shared with an individual student, a group of students, or the whole class. Teachers can turn to the exact page in the book to find the GTL examples to use "in the moment".
- *GTL to Use When Talking and Communicating with Parents* provide teachers with a GTL template for phone conversations, emails, or other types of messages to help transform parent relationships.
- *GTL Classroom Activities* provide teachers with classroom activities that bring GTL to life as students role-play GTL scenarios, participate in Hit the Pause Button Discussions, and revisit the Classroom Rules and Behavior Expectations together.

At the end of the book, we have also included an *Index of GTL Student Behavior Scenarios* that lists the 34 student behavior scenarios in Chapters 4 through 9.

In Chapter 10, we describe the Great Classroom Culture (GCC) which is built on the 11 GTL Word Categories. We present the GCC Framework, which describes the transformational outcomes that students and parents can experience when a teacher promotes the 11 GTL Word Categories in their classroom. We provide descriptions of the 11 GTL Word Categories and powerful GTL Combinations that promote and support a GCC. We also share how a GCC can break the burnout-to-dropout cycle; prevent student, parent, and teacher burnout; and promote vitality for you and your school community!

This book is a guide for transforming student behavior, parent relationships, and your classroom culture. It is our greatest hope that this book will become yours and become one of the favorite books in your personal library. We hope it will become frayed, raggedy, taped together in places, and full of yellow highlights and post-it notes as you use it every day.

1

Great Teacher Language

The Right Words at the Right Time

We believe the right words at the right time can make all the difference. We call these right words at the right time Great Teacher Language. Great Teacher Language is great language all teachers can use. Great Teacher Language can transform student behavior, parent relationships, and your classroom culture!

Wow, did you hear that? Did you hear what that teacher said? Those words were absolutely great! What professional and inspirational teacher language! She used the right words at the right time. That student was about to (fill in the blank) and those right words at the right time made all the difference. Her great teacher language resonated with the student and served as a compass, providing clear and respectful guidance. The student listened to what the teacher said, and the student's behavior was impacted in a positive way.

We believe Great Teacher Language (GTL) is great language all teachers can use every day to make a difference with students and parents. As you read this book, you will find hundreds of GTL examples you can use every day to transform student behavior, parent relationships, and your classroom culture.

Words Matter and Great Words Really Matter

Our language is a word quilt that is made up of all the words that have been offered to us and shared with us throughout our lives. We have adopted language from teachers, parents, coaches, friends, colleagues, and others. Adopting and acquiring language from others are a significant part of who we are. How we choose to use those words will make a difference! *Words matter*.

The words we use do make a difference. They set expectations. They inspire. They resonate. They move others. They are spoken. They are written. They are heard. They are felt. They help us to understand each other. *Words matter!*

Our daily work as teachers is demonstrated by a combination of what we do and the words we say—our Language of Practice (LoP). What we say to students, what we say to parents, and what we say to ourselves constitute our LoP. Our LoP is a foundational and vital part of our teaching practice that can be honed and refined much like other skills of a trade. We, as teachers, believe that a renewed and intentional interest in the words we speak to students and parents will lead to transformational outcomes. *Our words matter!*

When teachers use great words in the form of GTL, those words will help students and parents feel cared for and understood. GTL blends accountability with respect and love. Teachers can set high expectations, offer grace and guidance, build relationships, and promote unity when they speak great words to students and their parents. GTL encourages and offers hope to students and parents all along the way. GTL can transform student behavior, parent relationships, and your classroom culture. *Great words really matter!*

Defining Great Teacher Language

GTL is a (1) **teacher's LoP** that (2) **resonates with others**, (3) **influences others**, and (4) **produces transformational outcomes**.

Great Teacher Language is a Teacher's Language of Practice

On any given day in any classroom across the world, teachers are using a combination of different words that make up their LoP. For teachers, our LoP has major implications on our daily instructional practice. Earlier, we mentioned that our LoP is a foundational and vital part of our professional practice that can be honed and refined much like other skills of a trade. When our daily LoP integrates and reflects GTL, it can transform student behavior, parent relationships, and your classroom culture.

Great Teacher Language Resonates with Others

GTL resonates with the heart. Sometimes, despite our best attempts to communicate and emotionally connect with students, our LoP can be ignored, seem irrelevant, and go in one ear and out the other without ever touching the heart. In this situation, our words make no emotional connection, have no effect on these students, and leave them feeling disconnected and unphased. GTL can create a meaningful and emotional connection with students. We believe that GTL has a resonating affective quality that can resonate with a student's heart. As GTL resonates with students' hearts, these previously unphased and disconnected students discover they can do things they never thought they could do. GTL can transform your classroom culture as it touches students' and parents' hearts and resonates throughout your classroom and beyond.

Great Teacher Language Influences Others

GTL positively influences the hearts and minds of students and parents. GTL influences and carefully guides students from being disrespectful, passively disengaged, and emotionally disconnected to becoming respectful, actively engaged, and emotionally connected. The influential quality of GTL motivates and leads students to make better choices for themselves. Your job has positioned you, as a teacher, in front of a select group of young people and their parents, and they are both influenced by you! They observe you and listen to you, and you have a significant opportunity to teach them, lead them, influence their lives, and develop relationships with them in a positive way. When

GTL is used consistently by teachers, we believe it can positively influence and transform student behavior, parent relationships, and your classroom culture.

Great Teacher Language Produces Transformational Outcomes

GTL produces transformational outcomes in student behavior, parent relationships, and classroom culture. These transformational outcomes can serve as a catalyst for creating a Great Classroom Culture (GCC) of accountability, encouragement, grace, guidance, high expectations, hope, love, relationships, respect, understanding, and unity. In a GCC, all your students and their parents can expect to experience love, grace, encouragement, guidance, and high expectations for everyone's success. The more GTL is used with students and parents, the more people hear it and are transformed by it. This cycle of transformation feeds on itself and generates excitement, enthusiasm, vitality, and a confidence that success is possible for everyone!

In this chapter, we outlined the definition of GTL and highlighted how GTL can transform student behavior, parent relationships, and your classroom culture. As we all work to find the "right words at the right time," we strongly believe that GTL will lead to significant and transformational outcomes for you, your students, and their parents.

Chapter 2 will introduce two GTL Frameworks: one for transforming student behavior in the classroom and beyond and one for transforming parent relationships. Each GTL Framework is composed of the 11 GTL Word Categories that make up GTL. Chapter 2 will also provide definitions of the 11 GTL Word Categories and specific GTL examples to use with students and parents.

2

The 11 Great Teacher Language Word Categories and Frameworks for Transforming Student Behavior and Parent Relationships in the Classroom and Beyond

This chapter describes the Great Teacher Language (GTL) Frameworks for Transforming Student Behavior and Parent Relationships and the positive impact they can have on teachers, students, and parents. Each GTL Framework is composed of the 11 GTL Word Categories that make up GTL. Both GTL Frameworks highlight the power of GTL and the transformational purpose for using GTL. The GTL Frameworks for Transforming Student Behavior and Parent Relationships serve as a significant starting point for revisiting our teacher language and provide teachers with a reflective model for turning their Language of Practice into GTL.

The 11 Great Teacher Language (GTL) Word Categories offer guidance to teachers who are working to transform student behavior and parent relationships. The 11 GTL Word Categories are Words of Accountability, Words of Encouragement, Words of Grace, Words of Guidance, Words of High Expectations, Words of Hope, Words of Love, Words of Relationships, Words of Respect, Words of Understanding, and Words of Unity. In this chapter, we have provided specific definitions of the 11 GTL Word Categories for both students and parents. Under each GTL Word Category, you will find two GTL examples that are specific for both students and parents. We have included the ultimate behavior goal for students and the ultimate partnership goal for parent relationships for each GTL Word Category. Additionally, you will find hundreds of GTL examples you can use with students and parents in Chapters 3 to 9.

Words of Accountability

Definition for Students
Words of Accountability call for students to provide an account for their choices. They encourage and remind students that they are responsible to someone or for something. They address a problem "in the moment" and hold students accountable all along the way!

GTL Examples for Students

> "Jamie, that behavior is unacceptable and it's not how we agreed to treat each other when we set up our classroom expectations for how to respect one another."
> Words of Accountability

> "It is my job to help you understand that you have choices, and you will have to accept responsibility for those choices."
> Words of Accountability

> Goal for Students: Students reach personal accountability.

Definition for Parents
Words of Accountability provide parents a clear and respectful account of their child's classroom behaviors.

GTL Examples for Parents

> "Since the first day of school, we have been talking about respectful behaviors in the classroom and the importance

of showing respect to one another. I'm calling you to share something that happened today. Jamie was calling other students names and making fun of them in the classroom."

Words of Accountability

"At the beginning of the school year at the parent open house, you and I talked about the importance of maintaining a strong relationship and open communication between home and school. That's why I'm calling to share something that happened in class today. Jamie hit another student in our class.

The first thing I did was to speak to both students to get an understanding of what happened."

Words of Accountability

> Goal for Parents: Parents become well-informed supporters of their child and the teacher.

Words of Encouragement

Definition for Students
Words of Encouragement are specific and supportive words that rally students to overcome fears and failure and to "try, try again." These words inspire students with the desire, courage, and confidence to do the right thing for themselves and others. They are words that convey "I believe in you!"

GTL Examples for Students

"I know you are still struggling with your reading, but every day you are working harder and harder and you are improving. We will continue to work together, and I believe that by the end of the year, you will be caught up with the skills you need to be successful next year."

Words of Encouragement

"I appreciate how you waited to speak and gave the other students your attention while they were speaking. That was an act of respect for others."
Words of Encouragement

> Goal for Students: Students live a better way: to be all they can be.

Definition for Parents
Words of Encouragement inspire parents with positive support and encouragement.

GTL Examples for Parents

"I enjoy having Jamie in my class. He is (share something personal, positive, and specific that you've experienced with Jamie)."
Words of Encouragement

"I'm calling you and excited to share something that I noticed today at school. Jamie has been so excited about what we are learning in science this week. He has been asking questions, sharing information he has learned on his own, and motivating his classmates to learn more, too."
Words of Encouragement

> Goal for Parents: Parents feel encouraged about their child and their child's school experiences.

Words of Grace

Definition for Students
Words of Grace demonstrate love, patience, and respect for students despite what they do. They help us acknowledge that "we

all make mistakes," "nobody's perfect," and "forgive and forget." These words are not antagonistic, do not harbor ill feelings, and give students another chance to get it right!

GTL Examples for Students

> (Student returns from an out-of-school suspension for a defiant act toward you.) "We missed you—I am glad you are back."
>
> Words of Grace

> "When someone does something to hurt your feelings, it is important to talk with them about it. Once you have discussed it with them and they have apologized—let's all promise to forgive and forget."
>
> Words of Grace

> Goal for Students: Students experience and practice the power of forgiveness.

Definition for Parents

Words of Grace show parents you offer all students another chance to get it right and forgive their past mistakes.

GTL Examples for Parents

> "I'm looking forward to meeting with you and working together for Jamie. Although he has not been completing his work, he has plenty of time to catch up and get back on track. I will be helping him all along the way."
>
> Words of Grace

> "Thank you for talking with me today. I want to get to the root of Jamie's behavior and for him to know that I'm not upset with him and I care about him. However, his

behavior today was not acceptable and hopefully together we can help him avoid that type of behavior in the future."
Words of Grace

> Goal for Parents: Parents see and hear the power of forgiveness and second chances for their child.

Words of Guidance

Definition for Students
Words of Guidance give students a positive and supportive path to appropriate behavior, strong character, and success. They offer students advice— "Next time do/try this …. Consider this …. Here's another way." These words offer students an opportunity to improve and provide direction and assistance to the destination.

GTL Examples for Students

"If you find yourself having a moment when you really want to say something that you shouldn't—stop—think of all of the other possibilities—and choose your words carefully."
Words of Guidance

"If you need somebody to talk to or you've got a problem that you think might cause you to act out in class, then come pull me to the side one-on-one before we get class started."
Words of Guidance

> Goal for Students: Students practice self-management.

Definition for Parents
Words of Guidance inform parents of the guidance and assistance you and the school will provide to their child.

GTL Examples for Parents

> "We are teaching students the difference between using their cell phones for classroom lessons or an emergency versus using it for personal texting, video games, or social media. Cell phones can be a great tool for learning in class, but they can also be a huge distraction for students' learning."
>
> Words of Guidance

> "We are teaching students that it's so important to respect other students' belongings. They need to remember that what their other classmates have is not theirs, and if they would like to see it or use it, they need to ask for permission. Our goal is to promote mutual respect in our classroom."
>
> Words of Guidance

Goal for Parents: Parents are confident their child is supported and will receive the personalized guidance and assistance they need throughout the year.

Words of High Expectations

Definition for Students
Words of High Expectations demonstrate a belief in every student's ability to meet the highest levels of personal conduct and success. These words set high expectations and convey the anticipation that all students will meet them. They overcome low expectations and prejudgments. They help students to envision and pursue their best!

GTL Examples for Students

"I was so glad to see how you acted in our assembly today. You showed that you know how to pay attention and be a role model for other students. I'm excited to see you do the same thing in our classroom."
Words of High Expectations

"I'm excited for you to share your story with the class. We want to hear what you have to say. I know you can do this."
Words of High Expectations

> Goal for Students: Students achieve their full potential.

Definition for Parents

Words of High Expectations demonstrate to parents how you will help their child envision and pursue their best schoolwork and behavior.

GTL Examples for Parents

"My goal is to keep you informed about what Jamie is doing each week, so you can all know what to expect from me. I'll give Jamie his weekly folder to bring home, and you can access his weekly activities and progress updates through our school's website (or your school's learning management portal)."
Words of High Expectations

"Jamie has such a natural curiosity about science, and he is always so attentive in science class. He is such a great role model for the other students in our classroom. I am so proud of him and his desire to learn. I see Jamie having a job in science one day!"
Words of High Expectations

> Goal for Parents: Parents will expect their child to achieve their full potential both in school and at home.

Words of Hope

Definition for Students

Words of Hope inspire us to see others and the world with great potential. These words empower students to dream and achieve more! They instill the confidence that what is hoped for can happen! They also spark interests and ignite passions for learning!

GTL Examples for Students

> "My hope for all of you this year is that you learn how to manage your own behavior and make choices that are the right thing to do."
>
> Words of Hope

> "I am going to do my best to make learning as interesting and enjoyable as possible. Coming to our classroom every day will be like going on an adventure where you will be learning new things and enjoying yourself as you learn."
>
> Words of Hope

> Goal for Students: Students hope for—and work for—a better tomorrow.

Definition for Parents

Words of Hope inspire parents to look beyond the current circumstances and expect greater things for their child.

GTL Examples for Parents

"If you can think of anything we can do to make things even better for Jamie this year, please let me know. My hope is for all our students to feel safe, enjoy school, and learn as much as they can every day."

Words of Hope

"This year is going to be a great year for Jamie. There's so much to learn in (specific grade), and I'm going to be here to help him and keep you informed all along the way."

Words of Hope

> Goal for Parents: Parents experience ongoing hope for their child throughout the school year.

Words of Love

Definition for Students

Words of Love demonstrate an awareness that everyone needs to be loved, cared for, and valued. These words inspire students to use their words, talents, and gifts to help others. These words of love should never be confused with a "romantic love," nor should they be without accountability. Instead, these words are caring and supportive *with* accountability—the foundation for a strong relationship. They demonstrate the patience to endure students' misbehavior, an unwavering commitment, and a belief that students can improve!

GTL Examples for Students

"I believe in each one of you. Even though you might not think you can do this, I believe you can and I am here to help all of you. Do not hesitate to ask for help or to come to me for advice. My job is to be here for you and give you the care and attention you need."

Words of Love

> "Wait a second. Let me stop what I'm doing because I really want to listen to you."
>
> Words of Love

> Goal for Students: Students experience and practice the selfless power and purpose of putting others first.

Definition for Parents
Words of Love touch parents' hearts and demonstrate love and care for them and their child unconditionally.

GTL Examples for Parents

> "I wanted you to know that I encourage students to let me know when they need something they might have forgotten at home that day, like pencils, paper, a snack, and other things they might need."
>
> Words of Love

> "Jamie and your family are very important to me. If you can think of anything we can do to make things better for Jamie this year, please let me know."
>
> Words of Love

> Goal for Parents: Parents know without a doubt their child will experience unconditional care and receive loving accountability throughout the year.

Words of Relationship

Definition for Students
Words of Relationship help to maintain an emotionally safe and secure environment where students trust you and know where they stand. These words demonstrate a desire to relate to students

and to work with students to break down walls, build bridges, and reach common ground! They establish and nurture meaningful bonds with students by showing them they are "worth it"— they are valued and worth your time and your effort! Use these words when you talk with students individually—"heart to heart."

GTL Examples for Students

"I am so excited to get to know each of you this year, and I want you to get to know me, so let me tell you something about myself."

Words of Relationship

(Individual conversation with student who has been angry and disrespectful)

"If you are feeling angry when you get to school, you need to come and tell me. We can decide together how to solve your problem."

Words of Relationship

> Goal for Students: Students develop positive lifelong relationships with others.

Definition for Parents
Words of Relationship establish a trusting, caring, respectful, and positive connection with every parent.

GTL Examples for Parents

"At the beginning of the school year at the parent open house, we talked about the importance of maintaining a strong relationship and open communication between home and school. That's why I called today to share this update about Jamie."

Words of Relationship

"I've been talking to Jamie and working with him individually, and I also need your insight and influence and help. Could we meet sometime this week and sit down together to design a plan for Jamie? Together, we can get him the support he needs to be successful."

Words of Relationship

> Goal for Parents: Parents experience the power of a positive and transformational relationship with you and the school.

Words of Respect

Definition for Students
Words of Respect demonstrate a proper regard for the dignity of one's character and the character of others. These words convey an intentional, careful consideration and appreciation of others. Words of respect acknowledge the value of all people.

GTL Examples for Students

"It is so important to respect others by listening when they are speaking in class."

Words of Respect

"It's so important to respect other students' belongings. We need to remember that what your other classmates have is not yours, and if you would like to see it or use it, you will need to ask their permission."

Words of Respect

> Goal for Students: Students model respect for self and others.

Definition for Parents
Words of Respect demonstrate an intentional consideration and appreciation for all parents.

GTL Examples for Parents

"Hello! My name is .... I'm Jamie's teacher. He's not in trouble. Is now a good time for us to talk?"
Words of Respect

"I also want to share my contact information with you (share your school contact information) and let you know I'm available to answer any questions or concerns you have this year. I look forward to working with you and getting to know you this year."
Words of Respect

> Goal for Parents: Parents feel respected and valued by you.

Words of Understanding

Definition for Students
Words of Understanding demonstrate a conscious and deliberate effort to understand someone else's perspective by putting yourself in their position, putting yourself in their shoes, seeing things through their eyes, and hearing things through their ears. When individual student issues arise, these words demonstrate the desire to truly understand "what's going on" with the student by asking thoughtful questions that get to the root of the problem.

GTL Examples for Students

"Help me understand why you're so angry with (another student). We need to get to the bottom of this issue—so we can focus on our lesson. I'm wondering if it's a complete misunderstanding."
Words of Understanding

(A student continually says, "I am not going to do this work.")

"Can you help me understand what it is about this work that keeps you from doing it? Is it too hard? Too easy? Are you not interested in it? Let's take some time now to work out a plan for helping you to do your work in our classroom."

Words of Understanding

> Goal for Students: Students experience and practice empathy for others.

Definition for Parents

Words of Understanding demonstrate your desire to truly understand the parents' perspective.

GTL Examples for Parents

"Jamie didn't seem to want to talk with me about it, so I wanted to reach out to you to get a better understanding of how he's feeling about school and his work. Is there anything you can share or that you've heard him say that would help me know how to encourage Jamie with his schoolwork?"

Words of Understanding

"So I wanted to reach out and make you aware of his behavior and work together to get to the bottom of what is going on with Jamie. Has Jamie shared anything with you about our class, or other students in our class, that could give us a better understanding of how he's feeling about school? If he shares more with you while he's home, please let me know. I really want to understand what caused this and how to keep it from happening again."

Words of Understanding

> Goal for Parents: Parents are heard, understood, and valued as vital partners in ensuring their child's success.

Words of Unity

Definition for Students
Words of Unity transform a group of individuals into a team culture. These words encourage a "sense of belonging" and make it clear to all students that their presence and participation in classroom activities are valuable to the team. They also establish and promote a network of support in the classroom and beyond.

GTL Examples for Students

> "When we have problems in our classroom, we are going to talk and work together to reach a solution so in the end everyone is saying, 'Yes, that was a good way to solve that problem'."
>
> Words of Unity

> "Let's talk about the rules and behavior expectations for our classroom this year. What rules do we need for our classroom? Once we all agree on these rules and behavior expectations, I will ask your parents to sign that they agree with them. Then we will all be on the same page."
>
> Words of Unity

> Goal for Students: Students practice transformational teamwork through collaboration, agreement, and cooperation.

Definition for Parents
Words of Unity create a transformational culture of collaboration and teamwork with all parents.

GTL Examples for Parents

"Today in class, we worked together to develop our rules and behavior expectations for our classroom, and we created an agreement page for students, parents, and me to sign. Jamie will bring it home for you to sign and return to school. Our goal is for understanding and agreement for everyone."

Words of Unity

"I want to build a relationship with Jamie and your family this year. Our working together will help support his overall success in school."

Words of Unity

> Goal for Parents: Parents become personally engaged members of your classroom team.

The Great Teacher Language Framework for Transforming Student Behavior in the Classroom and Beyond

Table 2.1 presents the GTL Framework for Transforming Student Behavior in the Classroom and Beyond. This GTL framework has four columns and 11 rows. Each row represents the transformational impacts of using the GTL Word Categories with students.

The first column is the "Instead of" column. The "Instead of" column describes teacher behaviors that are sometimes used in the classroom. However, these "Instead of" behaviors often result in teacher and/or student frustration, unproductive outcomes, short-term solutions, or teacher and student burnout.

The second column and the anchor of the framework is the "Use" column. The "Use" column lists the 11 GTL Word Categories that can lead to transformational outcomes with students. These 11 GTL Word Categories provide a bridge between the "Instead of" column and the "To" column. For example,

TABLE 2.1 The Great Teacher Language Framework for Transforming Student Behavior in the Classroom and Beyond

Instead of	Use	To	So That Students
Allowing students to be irresponsible	Words of Accountability	Hold them accountable all along the way	Reach personal accountability
Unintentionally allowing students to become discouraged	Words of Encouragement	Rally students with the courage to overcome challenges, obstacles, barriers, failures, defeats, fears, apathy, etc.	Live a better way and become all they can be
Harboring ill feelings like unforgiveness and blame	Words of Grace	Separate the student from the behavior, forgive their past mistakes, and give them another chance to get it right	Experience and practice the power of forgiveness and second chances
Hoping that students find their way	Words of Guidance	Help students find a path to success and appropriate behavior	Practice self-management
Unintentionally discouraging and limiting students with low expectations	Words of High Expectations	Help students envision and pursue their best	Achieve their full potential
Surviving for today	Words of Hope	Inspire a vision of a better tomorrow	Hope for and work for a better tomorrow
Speaking only to the minds of our students	Words of Love	Touch their hearts and demonstrate love and care unconditionally	Experience and practice the selfless power and purpose of putting others first

(*Continued*)

TABLE 2.1 Continued

Instead of	Use	To	So That Students
Focusing only on the course content	**Words of Relationship**	Establish a caring and positive connection with each student	Develop positive lifelong relationships with others
Allowing a climate of disrespect in your classroom	**Words of Respect**	Demonstrate mutual admiration for one another	Model respect for self and others
Making assumptions based upon your perspective	**Words of Understanding**	Discover the student's perspective	Experience and practice empathy for others
Doing everything by yourself	**Words of Unity**	Nurture a culture of collaboration and teamwork in your classroom	Practice transformational teamwork through collaboration, agreement, and cooperation

"Instead of" unintentionally allowing students to become discouraged, "Use" Words of Encouragement "To" rally students with the courage to overcome challenges, obstacles, barriers, failures, defeats, fears, apathy, and so on.

The third column is the "To" column. The "To" column describes great teacher behaviors and transformational practices to use with students! For example, great teachers "Use" Words of Guidance "To" help students find a path to success and appropriate behavior.

The fourth column of the framework is the "So That Students" column. The "So That Students" column describes the student behavior goals and the student behavior transformations that are possible when we use GTL! For example, "Instead of" harboring ill feelings like unforgiveness and blame, "Use" Words of Grace "To" separate the student from the behavior, forgive their past mistakes, and give them a second chance to get it right "So that Students" experience and practice the power of forgiveness and second chances!

The Great Teacher Language Framework for Transforming Parent Relationships

Table 2.2 presents the GTL Framework for Transforming Parent Relationships. This GTL framework has four columns and 11 rows. Each row represents the transformational impacts of using the GTL Word Categories with parents.

The first column is the "Instead of" column. The "Instead of" column describes teacher behaviors that are sometimes used with parents. However, these "Instead of" behaviors often result in teacher and/or parent frustration, unproductive outcomes, short-term solutions, or teacher and parent burnout.

The second column and the anchor of the framework is the "Use" column. The "Use" column lists the 11 GTL Word Categories that can lead to transformational outcomes with parents. These 11 GTL Word Categories provide a bridge between the "Instead of" column and the "To" column. For example, "Instead of" unintentionally allowing parents to become discouraged,

TABLE 2.2 The Great Teacher Language Framework for Transforming Parent Relationships

Instead of	Use	To	So That Parents
Allowing parents to be uninformed or misinformed about classroom issues	**Words of Accountability**	Provide parents a clear and respectful account of their child's classroom behaviors	Become well-informed supporters of their child and the teacher
Unintentionally allowing parents to become discouraged	**Words of Encouragement**	Inspire parents with positive support and encouragement	Feel encouraged about their child and their child's school experiences
Allowing parents to experience a classroom culture of unforgiveness and blame	**Words of Grace**	Show parents you offer all students another chance to get it right and forgive their past mistakes	See and hear the power of forgiveness and second chances for their child
Hoping parents find the guidance and assistance they need to support their child's success	**Words of Guidance**	Inform parents of the guidance and assistance you and the school will provide to their child	Are confident their child is supported and will receive the personalized guidance and assistance they need throughout the year
Discouraging parents by having low expectations for their child	**Words of High Expectations**	Demonstrate to parents how you will help their child envision and pursue their best schoolwork and behavior	Will expect their child to achieve their full potential both in school and at home
Allowing parents to feel discouraged about their child's current school situation	**Words of Hope**	Inspire parents to look beyond the current circumstances and expect greater things for their child	Experience ongoing hope for their child throughout the school year

11 Great Teacher Language Word Categories and Frameworks ◆ 29

	Category		
Speaking only to the minds of parents	**Words of Love**	Touch parents' hearts and demonstrate love and care for them and their child unconditionally	Know without a doubt their child will experience unconditional care and receive loving accountability throughout the year
Focusing only on providing parents with facts and information	**Words of Relationship**	Establish a trusting, caring, respectful, and positive connection with every parent	Experience the power of a positive and transformational relationship with you and the school
Responding to parents disrespectfully	**Words of Respect**	Demonstrate an intentional consideration and appreciation for all parents	Feel respected and valued by you
Making assumptions about parents based on your perspective	**Words of Understanding**	Demonstrate your desire to truly understand the parents' perspective	Are heard, understood, and valued as vital partners in ensuring their child's success
Doing everything by yourself, without parents	**Words of Unity**	Create a transformational culture of collaboration and teamwork with all parents	Become personally engaged members of your classroom team

"Use" Words of Encouragement "To" inspire parents with positive support and encouragement.

The third column is the "To" column. The "To" column describes great teacher behaviors and transformational practices to use with parents! For example, great teachers "Use" Words of Guidance "To" inform parents of the guidance and assistance you and the school will provide their child.

The fourth column of the framework is the "So That Parents" column. The "So That Parents" column describes the parent relationship goals and relationship transformations that are possible when we use GTL! For example, "Instead of" allowing parents to experience a classroom culture of unforgiveness and blame, "Use" Words of Grace "To" show parents you offer all students another chance to get it right and forgive their past mistakes "So that Parents" see and hear the power of forgiveness and second chances for their child!

Great Teacher Language Frameworks for Transformation

The more you use these GTL Frameworks and integrate these GTL Word Categories and GTL examples into your daily teaching practice and make them your own, the more you will be able to transform student behavior, parent relationships, and your classroom culture.

Chapter 3 strategically focuses on GTL you can use on the first day of school with students and parents. Chapters 4 to 9 present challenging classroom behavior scenarios. Each chapter begins with the question 'What Do Great Teachers Say?' and identifies four to seven specific student behavior scenarios that are common in today's classrooms. In each chapter, you'll also find relevant and helpful background information related to each classroom behavior scenario. All of these chapters offer teacher-friendly charts with *GTL Reminders to Self*, *GTL to Share with Students*, *GTL to Use When Talking and Communicating with Parents*, and *GTL Whole Class Activities*. At the end of the book, we have included an *Index of GTL Student Behavior Scenarios* that lists the 34 student behavior scenarios in Chapters 4 to 9.

3

What Do Great Teachers Say on the First Day of School and the Days that Follow?

It's the first day of school and you're excited to meet your new students and learn with them. This first day and the days that follow give you an opportunity to get to know them, for them to get to know you, and for the students to get to know each other. This chapter provides teacher-friendly charts with Great Teacher Language (GTL) Reminders to Self, GTL to Share with Students, GTL to Use When Talking and Communicating with Parents, and GTL Classroom Activities specifically related to the following six GTL Classroom Culture Behavior Standards:

Standard 3.1: Setting High Expectations for All
Standard 3.2: Establishing the Rules and Behavior Expectations for Success
Standard 3.3: Creating a Culture of Community and Teamwork
Standard 3.4: Encouraging Self-Management
Standard 3.5: Leading by Example
Standard 3.6: Building Relationships with Students and Their Families

> We know these are not the only classroom behavior standards that you will communicate to your students on the first day of school and the days that follow. These specific classroom behavior standards are a starting point for you to develop your Great Teacher Language (GTL) for your classroom on the first day and every day. For some of our classroom behavior standards, we have included GTL examples for you to use when talking and communicating with parents. These GTL examples are templates for phone conversations, emails, or other types of messages to develop strong communication between teachers and parents and to promote understanding, relationships, trust, and collaboration.

On the first day of school with a classroom full of students, your words can make all the difference. Some students are excited about what's in store, others are nervous and anxious, while others were perfectly happy with their summer vacation and are now quite disappointed and apathetic about being back in school. Acknowledging and addressing these first-day feelings of excitement, anxiety, fear, uncertainty, disappointment, and apathy constitute perhaps a teacher's first challenge—or opportunity—to connect with each student on a personal level. A teacher's Language of Practice (LoP) in the form of GTL during these first days sets the tone, provides direction, and conveys expectations of what is to come. These initial words embody the teacher's beliefs and values and provide an example of what the teacher expects to see and hear from all students. Your GTL establishes standards and structures that promote a safe and secure environment, both physically and emotionally, and can offer your new students the accountability, encouragement, grace, guidance, high expectations, hope, love, relationships, respect, understanding, and unity they need to begin and continue the best school year yet.

Setting High Expectations for All

Setting high expectations for students begins on the first day of school. The high expectations that teachers convey to all their students can propel each of them closer to reaching their potential. What if these high expectations are presented without encouragement and clear guidance? Sometimes, students hear high expectations but don't have a personal map or the tools to get there. Telling students "You can do anything you set your mind to" can be confusing for a student who has never experienced success or who has a discipline folder full of past mistakes. This confusion can be addressed with a consistent language that offers real hope with real guidance. What do you expect of your students? What do you want your students to expect of you? How will you offer encouragement and guidance to help students reach their potential?

The following GTL examples offer words that teachers can use on their first day of school and in the days that follow to set high expectations for both students and themselves. Within these language examples, you will find GTL Words of Encouragement, Words of Grace, Words of Guidance, and Words of Hope. Weaving these additional GTL words into your Words of High Expectations can provide the support your students need to reach their potential this year.

WHAT DO GREAT TEACHERS SAY WHEN...?

Setting High Expectations for All (Classroom Behavior Standard 3.1)
GTL Reminders to Self:

Remember... To keep encouragement alive in your classroom and provide daily opportunities for student success.
Words of Encouragement

Remember... Have high expectations for every child who walks through that door.
Words of High Expectations

Remember... A classroom filled with hope brings energy to the students and the teacher.
Words of Hope

Remember... Setting high expectations for your students begins on the first day of school.
Words of Guidance

Remember... Offer each student a fresh start to their new school year.

Words of Grace

Remember... There is wisdom in reviewing a student's past academic and behavior records, but don't let their past mistakes define them this year.

Words of Grace

GTL to Share with Students:

"This year, we are going to be learning some difficult things, but I am excited about helping each of you learn as much as you can. Even if you think you can't learn in my classroom, I am going to work hard to change your mind!"

Words of Encouragement

"The 'not so good' things you did in the past don't have to affect what you do this year. We are all going to have a fresh start!"

Words of Grace

"Each of you has strengths and talents. As I get to know you this year, my job will be to help you discover them and use them to do well this year."

Words of Guidance

"I am so excited about this new school year. I have always loved school, and I have always loved to learn. It is my greatest hope that you will love learning, too!"

Words of Hope

"I expect a lot from each of you, and I want you all to expect a lot from me. Let's talk about what you expect from me as your teacher."

Words of High Expectations

"It's going to be a great school year because you are a great group of students."

Words of High Expectations

> "I am going to do my best to make learning as interesting and enjoyable as possible. Coming to our classroom every day will be like going on an adventure where you will be learning new things and enjoying yourself as you learn."
>
> Words of Hope
>
> "We want our classroom to be filled with encouragement for one another. Let's remember to encourage each other with our words and actions."
>
> Words of Encouragement

Establishing Rules and Behavior Expectations for Success

On the first day of school, it is essential that you establish rules and behavior expectations **with** your students. As you and your students discuss (1) possible rules for their classroom, (2) what they expect of you as their teacher, and (3) what you can expect of them as students, it is important to involve all the students and value everyone's input. Student-generated behavior expectations for both the teacher and themselves—supported with teacher guidance—can almost guarantee student buy-in.

The rules and expectations for classroom behavior that you and your students speak into existence and the language used in your classroom will generate your classroom culture. Providing students with clear language examples of Words of Accountability, Words of Encouragement, Words of Grace, Words of Guidance, Words of High Expectations, Words of Hope, Words of Love, Words of Relationship, Words of Respect, Words of Understanding, and Words of Unity offers students an idea of how they can respond appropriately to situations before, during, and after they encounter them.

In fact, our hope is that schools provide the structure and guidelines that students need to practice self-management both in school and in the real world. What will the rules and behavior expectations "sound like" in your classroom? How will you facilitate a Classroom Rules and Behavior Expectations discussion that respects everyone's input and also incorporates your values and beliefs? How do you plan to encourage input from all students? What will you say if a student suggests an inappropriate rule? (At the end of this chapter, see GTL Classroom Activity entitled "Setting up the Rules and Behavior Expectations for the Classroom on the First Day of School".)

The first day of school is such a "blank slate." Our words are so important in creating and developing classroom rules and behavior expectations. Below are GTL examples to guide you and your students as you develop the rules and behavior expectations on the first day of school.

WHAT DO GREAT TEACHERS SAY WHEN...?

Establishing Rules and Behavior Expectations for Success (Classroom Behavior Standard 3.2)

GTL Reminders to Self:

Remember... Students do not need to guess what is right or wrong in the classroom. From Day 1, they need to know what the rules and behavior expectations are.

Words of High Expectations

Remember... Creating your rules and behavior expectations in a positive and collaborative way will ensure buy-in from your students.

Words of Love

Remember... From the very first day of class, allow students to have ownership in your classroom by working as a team to set up the classroom rules and behavior expectations. Encourage them to work together throughout the year, to maintain a safe and high standard of behavior expectations for everyone.

Words of Unity

Remember... During the first day of school, ask your students to write down or to share verbally their expectations of you as a teacher.

Words of High Expectations

Remember... Distractions and misbehaviors can mess up your lesson plan. It is important to "hit the pause button" on the lesson and seize opportunities to address these behaviors immediately by talking with the whole class about the issue. Addressing the misbehavior immediately may solve the discipline issue for the rest of the school year and sets the tone for your classroom behavior expectations.

See the GTL Classroom Activities (Hit the Pause Button) at the end of Chapters 4–9 for examples.

Words of Accountability

GTL to Share with Students:

"Let's talk about the rules and behavior expectations for our classroom this year. What rules do we need for our classroom? Once we all agree on these rules and behavior expectations, I will ask your parents to sign that they agree with them. Then we will all be on the same page."

Words of Unity

"It's important for all of you to know that I am going to hold everyone accountable to the same rules guidelines and behavior expectations."

Words of Accountability

"Our classroom rules and behavior expectations will help us get along better in school and outside of school."

Words of Guidance

"From time to time this year, I am going to have personal conferences with you. These conferences will be opportunities for you to share problems or concerns you have, and we can discuss what we can do together to help you be successful."

Words of Guidance

"Now that we've agreed on our rules and behavior expectations, let's talk about what each of these would 'sound like and look like.' What does respecting each other sound like and look like?"

Words of Respect

> "Before we move on, let's make sure that everyone understands what we have discussed. Does anyone have any questions about the rules and behavior expectations we have agreed on today?"
>
> Words of Understanding
>
> "Today, we are going to work together to develop our rules and behavior expectations for our classroom. Let's begin with everyone sharing their thoughts and ideas."
>
> Words of Unity
>
> "I want all of you to feel comfortable in this class. We have procedures and clear expectations to keep our classroom a safe place for all of us to learn."
>
> Words of Unity
>
> "You can expect me to treat all of you with respect and care."
>
> Words of Love

Creating a Culture of Community and Teamwork

Your GTL on the first day of school and the days that follow will lay the foundation for relationship building, team building, trust, and mutual respect. Creating a Great Classroom Culture of community and teamwork begins with a teacher who says, "I am willing to listen to you, and I want to know what you think." When students know that their voices are heard and valued, they feel connected—like they belong to something. Student input in the development of the classroom culture leads to unity, empowerment, a sense of belonging, teamwork, and collaboration. What classroom culture do you believe will be the most conducive to students' academic and social growth? Are you willing to encourage feedback and input from your students? How will your language encourage students to "join the team"?

Below are GTL examples to guide you and your students as you work together to create a culture of community and teamwork on the first day of school and the days that follow.

WHAT DO GREAT TEACHERS SAY WHEN…?

Creating a Culture of Community and Teamwork (Classroom Behavior Standard 3.3)

GTL Reminders to Self:

Remember… Your classroom needs to be a place where students thrive not just survive.
Words of Hope

Remember… Your job as a teacher is much like a musical conductor blending each individual student note into something harmonious.
Words of Unity

Remember… When students feel like they belong to something—in this case, the classroom community—they are more likely to work together as a team.
Words of Unity

Remember… There is a big difference between asking a student to do something and telling a student to do something. Asking students to be a part of a team demonstrates a level of respect; on the other hand, telling them they are going to be on a team suggests a demand.
Words of Respect

Remember… Instead of always saying 'No' to students who want to do something at an inappropriate time, consider a 'Yes with Guidance'. For example, when a group of students wants to go to the media center to work on a project, instead of saying, 'No, now is not the time to go to the media center', say 'Yes, your team can go right after lunch today.'
Words of Guidance

GTL to Share with Students:

"Now that we have discussed and decided on the rules and behavior expectations for our classroom, let's encourage each other to follow them."
Words of Encouragement

"We all make mistakes. At some point this year, everybody in this class—including me—will do something that causes us to feel embarrassed. Let's promise not to make fun of others when this happens, because that will make them feel more embarrassed."

Words of Respect

"When a new student joins our classroom, let's make sure we welcome them and make them feel comfortable."

Words of Respect

"My primary job is to teach you as much as I can this year, but I see myself as a learner too. I know there will be many times when I will learn a lot from you and what you have to say. I hope you will be both a learner and a teacher as well."

Words of Relationship

"This year, we are going to have classroom meetings. These meetings will be an opportunity for us to discuss problems and work together to come up with solutions."

Words of Unity

"We have behavior expectations for doing group work in our class. You'll get more done in your groups by following these behavior expectations together. Are there any questions you have about them—let's share those questions now so you won't come back and say, 'Our group doesn't know how to work together'."

Words of Guidance

"What are some positive things we want to happen in our classroom this year? Now for these things to happen, what do we all need to do? Let's come up with a list of the positive things we want to happen and another list for what we need to do to make them happen this year."

Words of Unity

"When we have problems in our classroom, we are going to talk and work together to reach a solution so in the end everyone is saying, 'Yes, that was a good way to solve that problem'."
Words of Unity

"How should we treat each other and talk to each other? Let's come up with a list of examples we can use this year."
Words of High Expectations

"In our classroom, we don't want anyone to feel embarrassed to ask questions or share their ideas. We will work together to respect each other's thoughts and ideas."
Words of Respect

"In our classroom, we are a team. We'll support each other, motivate each other, see things through others' eyes, hear things through others' ears, and respect each other."
Words of Unity

"We all agreed in our classroom meeting last week on how we will handle this specific group work problem we're having (e.g., who is going to be the group leader). So let's follow through with the decision we made together (e.g., we are going to rotate who will be leader)."
Words of Accountability

Encouraging Self-Management

Encouraging your students and guiding them to become self-managed people starts on the first day of school. When students learn to become self-managed, they choose to manage their own behavior without coercion or control from others. When we use our power and authority to coerce students into doing something, it might provide a short-term quick fix in your classroom now, but it doesn't empower students to choose to manage their own behavior in the moment or for their lifetime. Teacher language in the form of GTL sets the stage for an environment that helps students move from a mindset where "The teacher's making me do this" to "I'm doing this because I'm choosing to do it, and it's the right thing to do."

It is also important to promote a classroom environment where students understand that they have the freedom to choose their behaviors. Along with that freedom, however, they have to accept responsibility for those choices and realize the impact that their choices have on themselves, their future, and the people around them.

Below are GTL examples to use as you encourage and guide your students to become self-managed on the first day of school and the days that follow.

WHAT DO GREAT TEACHERS SAY WHEN...?

Encouraging Self-Management (Classroom Behavior Standard 3.4)

GTL Reminders to Self:

Remember... Remind your students every day of the importance of self-management, personal accountability, good behavior, and getting along with one another.
Words of Accountability

Remember... We encourage student self-management when we choose to persuade and help students adopt a pattern of good behavior over time, not when we coerce or punish them in the moment.
Words of Love

Remember... Your goal this year is to help each student become self-managed. A self-managed student has made a conscious choice to demonstrate good behavior both in public and in private.
Words of Guidance

Remember... When we use our power and authority to coerce students into doing something, it might provide a short-term quick fix, but it doesn't empower students to become self-managed.
Words of Guidance

GTL to Share with Students:

"If you have a problem with behavior this year, I am going to ask you how you plan to fix the situation."
Words of Accountability

"As your teacher, it's part of my job to help you understand that you have choices and that you will have to accept responsibility for those choices."
Words of Accountability

"If I have a problem with you, I am going to quickly bring it to your attention, and if you have a problem with me or any of your classmates, let us know as soon as possible. Let's address our concerns openly and honestly so we don't hold grudges."
Words of Grace

"Every day, you have a choice to decide what you will say, what you will do, how you will act, and how you will treat others."
Words of Guidance

"My goal for each of you is that you will learn how to make the right choices both in school and outside of school."
Words of Guidance

"My hope for all of you this year is that you learn how to manage your own behavior and make choices that are the right thing to do."
Words of Hope

"How you behave in our classroom will be your choice. We're going to discuss important choices you'll have to make throughout the year and come up with a list of those decisions and the consequences of the choices you make."
Words of Accountability

> "Throughout the year, you'll make choices that have consequences, and you'll already know the consequences that we've agreed on."
> Words of Accountability
>
> (When a student makes an inappropriate choice during the first days of school) "The choice you made (not to complete your work, for example) has a consequence. I really wish you had been able (to complete it or …), but because you chose not to, the consequence will be what we agreed on the first day of school, which is … (you will need to stay in from break to finish it, etc.)."
> Words of Accountability

Leading by Example

When teachers model appropriate language and actions, it gives clear direction to students. Modeling what you expect to hear and see from your students is the greatest way of leading by example and turning abstract concepts into concrete observable behaviors. Modeling an abstract concept like "respect" and discussing what it sounds like and looks like with your class help students learn how to demonstrate respect for themselves and others. (See GTL Classroom Activity "Hit the Pause Button for Discussion on Promoting Mutual Respect in the Classroom When You See Multiple Students Being Respectful" in Chapter 7.) During the first day of school and the days that follow, spend time discussing and role-playing with your students what difficult and ambiguous concepts sound like and look like. For example, encourage students to act out what grace and respect sound like and look like. Asking students for their input on how they would speak and act models for students your ability to respect their input and demonstrate grace when their responses need guidance. This culture of collaboration also models for students that "This is our classroom! Let's all agree on how we want to talk to one another and treat each other!"

It is important to model the behaviors you expect from your students and yourself every day. How are you going to model the behavior you hope to see? How will you model encouragement, grace, hope, love, and respect on the first day of school? We can miss the mark with students when we tell them to "show respect" without giving them specific examples of what respect looks like and sounds like. The following GTL examples illustrate what Words of Accountability, Words of Encouragement, Words of Grace, Words of Guidance, Words of High Expectations, Words of Hope, Words of Love, Words of Respect, and Words of Relationship will look like and sound like in the classroom.

WHAT DO GREAT TEACHERS SAY WHEN…?

Leading by Example (Classroom Behavior Standard 3.5)

GTL Reminders to Self:

Remember… Think carefully about your Language of Practice, the tone of your voice, the words themselves, what you want to convey, the outcome you desire to see, and what you hope to inspire.

Words of High Expectations

Remember… It is important to model hope for your students on the first day of school and the days that follow. When they see and hear you hoping for something and believing in something better, it gives them hope to do the same.

Words of Hope

Remember… When students see us modelling care for them, they are more likely to practice care for their classmates.

Words of Love

Remember… You are responsible for the tone you set for your classroom. Model what you want your students to do. Be respectful, be on time, and be prepared.

Words of Accountability

Remember... On the first day of school, explain to your students that you are going to respect them and that you expect them to respect you.

Words of Respect

Remember... You need to model and teach students how to respect each other and themselves, by showing them what respect looks like and sounds like.

Words of Guidance

Remember... Grace is a powerful way to show patience and love for others.

Words of Grace

GTL to Share with Students:

"We really need to think about what we say. Words do matter."

Words of Accountability

"It's my job to explain why we're learning what we're learning, so you can understand why it's important and then you can learn and do well in school this year."

Words of Encouragement

"In our class, we are going to practice grace—and grace is offering others something they might not deserve."

Words of Grace

"I am going to try my best to model grace for you. Grace is offering others another chance to get things right. At some point, you might blow it—and I'll offer grace and the support you need to do it better the next time."

Words of Grace

"I know I am not perfect and I'm going to make mistakes this year and when I do, I will be the first to apologize."

Words of Grace

"I want all of you to know I will be prepared for class every day and I expect all of you to be prepared, too."
                                      Words of High Expectations

"I want you all to know I won't expect anything of you I don't expect from myself. I will make sure I am in class on time, and I will follow our classroom rules."
                                      Words of High Expectations

"I am so excited to get to know each of you this year, and I want you to get to know me, so let me tell you something about myself."
                                                Words of Relationship

Building Relationships with Students and Their Families

In the classroom, relationships are everything! We believe a Great Classroom Culture starts with a genuine care for students and their families. Students need a teacher who cares about them, looks out for them, and guides them in love all along the way. This love is never to be confused with a "romantic love," nor should this love be without accountability. Instead, this love is a caring and supporting love **with** accountability—the foundation for a strong relationship.

    Teaching is a matter of the heart. The relationships you begin to develop with your students and their families on the first day and continue to nurture throughout the year set the stage for deep trust and understanding. When teachers intentionally make an effort to connect with each student individually, it tells the student, "You are important to me" and "I care about you." In addition, when teachers intentionally make an effort to connect with the student's family, it shows the student and their family, "Your family is important to me" and "I care about your family." We believe that getting to know students personally is a key to reaching them educationally. We also believe that a strong relationship with the student's family significantly impacts their overall success in school. The following GTL examples demonstrate an intentional desire to connect with students' hearts to build meaningful relationships.

WHAT DO GREAT TEACHERS SAY WHEN…?

Building Relationships with Students and Their Families (Classroom Behavior Standard 3.6)

GTL Reminders to Self:

Remember… Students need a teacher who wants the best for them and who is looking out for them and working to develop relationships with them and their families.

Words of Relationship

Remember… Teaching is a matter of the heart.

Words of Love

Remember… It's important for your classroom to be ready and welcoming on the first day of school, but it's your commitment to care for and connect with your students and their families that will make the biggest difference.

Words of Love

Remember… Strong relationships with students and their families impact the overall success of students in school.

Words of Relationship

Remember… Every student is unique, and you need to get to know each student individually.

Words of Understanding

Remember… Seize every opportunity to greet students with a smile and a kind word.

Words of Relationship

Remember… Look for opportunities to bond with your students. Walk with them, talk with them, eat with them, and laugh with them.

Words of Relationship

Remember… When you call, email, or text parents about a student behavior issue concerning their child, be positive and respectful while sharing the truth about the situation.

Words of Respect

GTL to Share with Students:

"I am here to help each one of you. Do not hesitate to ask for help or to come to me for advice. My job is to be here for you and give you the care and attention you need."

Words of Love

"I am going to treat you the same way I want to be treated."

Words of Respect

"Thanks for sharing (a piece of paper, a pencil) with your classmate today. That was very kind of you."

Words of Relationship

"I love and care about my students and their families. You and your family are important to me, and I look forward to working with all of you this year."

Words of Love

"I'm excited to meet all of you today! This year, we are going to be getting to know each other. I want to know what you're interested in, what you care about, and your favorite things to do."

Words of Relationship

"I am looking forward to getting to know your parents this year. I plan on staying in close contact with them so we can all help you be successful."

Words of Relationship

"We are all different and interesting in our own way. Some of us are outgoing, and some of us are quiet. Let's try to get to know each other better this year. We can learn a lot from our differences."
Words of Understanding

GTL to Use When Talking and Communicating with Parents:

Introductory phone call to the parents of your new students!
(Note: This GTL phone conversation provides a template you can modify and send to parents as a letter, email, text message, etc.).

"Hello! My name is …. I'm excited to be Jamie's teacher this year! Is now a good time for us to talk?"
Words of Respect

"I wanted to reach out and introduce myself so you know more about me." (Share some personal and professional information that helps to build a relationship with the parent.)
Words of Relationship

"This year is going to be a great year for Jamie. There's so much to learn in (specific grade), and I'm going to be here to help him and keep you informed all along the way."
Words of Hope

"I also want to share my contact information with you (share your school contact information) and let you know I'm available to answer any questions or concerns you have this year."
Words of Accountability

"Today in class, we worked together to develop our rules and behavior expectations for our classroom, and we created an agreement page for students, parents, and me to sign. Jamie will bring it home for you to sign

and return to school. Our goal is to have understanding and agreement for everyone."
Words of Unity

"Maintaining a strong relationship and open communication between home and school is essential to Jamie's success this year."
Words of Relationship

"My goal is to keep you informed about what Jamie is doing each week, so you can all know what to expect from me. I'll give Jamie his weekly folder to bring home, and you can access his weekly activities and progress updates through our school's website (or your school's learning management portal)."
Words of High Expectations

"Jamie and your family are important to me."
Words of Love

"I want to build a relationship with Jamie and your family this year. Our working together will help support his overall success in school."
Words of Unity

"If you can think of anything we can do to make things even better for Jamie this year, please let me know. My hope is for all our students to feel safe, enjoy school, and learn as much as they can every day."
Words of Hope

GTL Classroom Activities to Transform Student Behavior and Your Classroom Culture

GTL Classroom Activities for Students on the First Day of School and the Days That Follow

We see these activities as either "in the moment" on the first day of school or a time to circle up for classroom meetings on the days that follow, to encourage student voice and student engagement in your classroom. We see the teacher as a facilitator and co-learner during these GTL activities and students as active participants in learning how to "see the classroom through the lens of the teacher" and how to manage their own behavior.

1. (Role-play GTL Scenario Introduction on the First Day of School or on the Days that Follow.) Describe what a role-play is for the whole class. Tell them how you will pick different students to participate in each role-play. Explain how the whole class will be participating in specific role-plays to address discipline issues that happen from time to time. Share with students how important role-playing is for practicing how to respectfully act and treat each other in the classroom. Also, share with students how role-playing will help them understand and demonstrate what positive behaviors will sound like and look like. Start your first role-play activity. In this role-play, you (the teacher) will play yourself. This activity will allow you an opportunity to role-play how you will respectfully treat them (words and actions) when specific discipline issues occur in your classroom. Select two students to role-play a discipline issue such as texting on their cell phones to one another during a class lesson, or two students talking to one another while the teacher is trying to teach, or one student taking another student's pencil or belongings, and so on. As the teacher, you will respectfully address the issue by reminding the students of the rules and behavior expectations you all created together. Conclude the role-play by sharing with students that your respectful behavior (words and actions) is what they can expect from you as their teacher.
2. (Hit the Pause Button Introduction on the First Day of School or the Days that Follow for Positively Engaging Parents.) Describe what a Hit the Pause Button Discussion will look like for the whole class. Explain how you will "hit the pause button" to address discipline issues or other issues that happen from time to time. Share with students how important learning is and how your Hit the

Pause Button discussions are a quick way for addressing and resolving classroom issues and getting everyone back to the lesson. Start your first Hit the Pause Button Discussion. Share with the students that you are going to "Hit the Pause Button" on the lesson and take important time to discuss your goals for building positive relationships with their parents and families. Explain to the students that you look forward to getting to know their parents this year and how you will also be calling and/or communicating with their parents this week to introduce yourself. Also, share with students that you will be sending home weekly student work folders to keep their parents updated on their progress throughout the year. Remind students to share the Student/Teacher/Parent Agreement with their parents and return it to school. Emphasize the importance of teamwork where parents, students, and teachers will work together for the student's success.

Throughout the first days of school, you can Hit the Pause Button for other discussions:
- Hit the Pause Button Discussion for "Classroom Distractions" in Chapter 4.
- Hit the Pause Button Discussion for "When to Talk and When to Listen" in Chapter 5.
- Hit the Pause Button Discussion for "Why Do We Have to Learn This?" in Chapter 6.
- Hit the Pause Button Discussion on "Promoting Mutual Respect in the Classroom" in Chapter 7.
- Hit the Pause Button Discussion on "Encouraging Students' Management of Anger" in Chapter 8.
- Hit the Pause Button Discussion for "What Bullying Is and What to Do If You are Bullied" in Chapter 9.

3. (Setting up "Our Classroom Rules and Behavior Expectations" on the First Day of School and the Days that Follow.) Describe how you and the students will collaborate to develop a list of behavior expectations for each other and how all of you will collaborate to develop a list of your classroom rules for the year. Explain how

your teamwork approach is doing it "with them" and "not to them." The goal is to allow each student a chance to play an ownership role in the process and to share their thoughts and feelings on how everyone will act and treat each other in the classroom this year. Share with students the importance of agreeing on classroom behaviors and rules and following them so every student feels safe, enjoys school, and learns as much as they can every day. As the teacher, you will have a tentative list of behavior expectations and rules to guide the discussion. Start your discussion to determine "What You Can Expect from Me as Your Teacher and What I Can Expect from You as a Student". Ask your students to write down their expectations of you as their teacher or ask them to share their ideas verbally and make a class chart. Here is an example of a possible teacher behavior expectations list based on GTL.

As your teacher,
- I will respect and care for you.
- I will be prepared to teach you every day.
- I will not embarrass you in front of the class.
- I will be here to help you when you need me.
- I will listen to you and encourage you.
- I am going to challenge you to work hard and make good choices.
- I am going to teach you new things this year, and I'll help you learn them.
- I am going to always be looking for win-win solutions for every situation.
- I am going to connect with your parents this year.

Then spend some time creating the student behavior expectations list together.

The behavior expectations for the student list could include the following:

As a student,
- I will respect the teacher and other students.
- I will be prepared and try hard to learn something new every day.
- I will work to get along with everyone.

- I will not embarrass my classmates or my teacher.
- I will make good choices.
- I will focus on learning.
- I will pay attention during lessons.
- I will avoid distractions.
- If I need help, I'll ask for help.
- I will work for win-win solutions with the teacher and other students.

After you've discussed the behavior expectations for everyone, explain to students how your lists might grow throughout the year if new behavior expectations need to be added. The next part of the discussion will be using these behavior expectations lists to create your classroom rules together. Guide your students through the discussion and help them create rules that are appropriate for everyone. Once your classroom rules are agreed on, post them in the classroom where everyone can see them. Conclude the discussion by thanking all the students for working together to create the behavior expectations and rules. Remind students how you will share these rules and behavior expectations with their parents in the Student/Teacher/Parent Agreement. Their parents will sign the agreement and return it to the school.

We encourage you to use this same discussion format during the first days of school to set up your classroom rules and behavior expectations for other important issues and revisit them throughout the year. For example:
- Revisiting the Classroom Rules and Behavior Expectations for "Proper Cell Phone/Computer Use in the Classroom" in Chapter 4.
- Revisiting the Classroom Rules and Behavior Expectations for "Being Respectful to Others" in Chapter 5.
- Revisiting the Classroom Rules and Behavior Expectations for "Profanity" in Chapter 6.
- Revisiting the Classroom Rules and Behavior Expectations for "Respecting Other Students' Belongings" in Chapter 7.

- Revisiting the Classroom Rules and Behavior Expectations for "What You Can Expect from Me as Your Teacher and What I Can Expect from You as a Student" in Chapter 8.
- Revisiting the Classroom Rules and Behavior Expectations for "Clear Expectations for Behavior and the Consequences for Fighting and Bullying Behaviors" in Chapter 9.

4

What Do Great Teachers Say When a Student Is Passively Disengaged?

What do you say when you notice a student who is passively disengaged from the lesson (e.g., texting on their cell phone, sleeping, daydreaming, putting their head on their desk, or looking frustrated). This chapter provides teacher-friendly charts with Great Teacher Language (GTL) Reminders to Self, GTL to Share with Students, GTL to Use When Talking and Communicating with Parents, and GTL Classroom Activities specifically related to the following:

Scenario 4.1: A student is texting on his cell phone or scrolling through his computer.
Scenario 4.2: A student is sleeping in class.
Scenario 4.3: A student is not working on his assignment and looks embarrassed, troubled, stressed and/or frustrated.
Scenario 4.4: A student is not paying attention to the lesson and is daydreaming in class.
Scenario 4.5: A student never verbally participates in class.
Scenario 4.6: A passively disengaged student has failing grades in your class.

> We know these are not the only passively disengaged student behaviors that happen in your classroom. These specific scenarios are a starting point for you to develop your Great Teacher Language (GTL) for your classroom. For some of our student behavior scenarios, we have included GTL examples for you to use when talking with parents. These GTL examples are templates for phone conversations, emails, or other types of messages to develop strong communication between teachers and parents and to promote understanding, relationships, trust, and collaboration.

Disengaged students present an interesting dilemma. While their behavior is usually not a disruption to others or the lesson, it is not acceptable behavior for the classroom. There is a tendency to ignore these students because they are not bothering anyone. However, their behavior is communicating something to us, and they need our help and guidance. When teachers address these passive behaviors to meet the individual student's needs, it not only helps the disengaged student but also prevents the rest of the classroom from assuming that the behaviors are acceptable. Your Language of Practice (LoP) in the form of GTL can offer these passively disengaged students the accountability, encouragement, grace, guidance, high expectations, hope, love, relationships, respect, understanding, and unity necessary to successfully engage them in the learning.

Telling disengaged students to stop a certain behavior addresses the problem for the moment, but it is important to get to the root of the problem as well. Your words can help many passively disengaged students see the relevance and importance of staying engaged, interested, and involved so they can choose to behave appropriately. Your language can also help other students, who have personal issues, get the additional counselling and support they need. Your LoP in the form of GTL should demonstrate to students that what you teach is relevant, you expect their involvement, and you want to help them stay engaged in learning.

When students are disengaged, there is a tendency for us to react in a way to preserve our pride, dignity, and control. There is a big difference between a teacher exclaiming, "You don't need to be sleeping in my class!" as opposed to pulling the student aside privately and asking, "Is everything ok—I noticed that you were sleeping in class?" We need to carefully take our pride out of the equation and really pursue the student's needs and try to understand the student's perspective. Why are they sleeping in class? Why are they texting on their phone? Why are they choosing certain behaviors instead of paying attention to the lesson? By separating the student from their behavior, we start to get a different picture of the circumstances surrounding the student's behavior. That's not to say that their behavior will be accepted in the classroom. However, when we have insight into why students are making certain choices, we get closer to understanding how to help them make better choices. When you are not angry with yourself—not angry with the student—it provides a clearer perspective for getting to the root of the problem.

Many kids don't get it. They don't see the value in school today or the value of an education for a lifetime. So many other fun and exciting technological distractions are much more interesting to them. It's no wonder that students are saying—or thinking—"School is sooooo boring!" These distractions make the disengaged and passive students more difficult to reach. There is a whole world of real and virtual experiences that make schools appear less exciting and enjoyable. How can schools compete with that?

Often teachers feel the pressure to engage students by making everything fun and exciting. Lights, camera, action, fun! But when the fun ends, the students tune out. Other teachers plan lessons that attempt to meet all students' interests, but is that really possible all the time? The one thing teachers can do is to make their content relevant to all students. When teachers connect "the student's world" to the "world at large," the classroom lessons become more relevant, meaningful, helpful, valuable, and important to the students. This approach enables the disengaged and passive students in your classroom to see "why they need to learn this information" and "how it's going to help them today and in the future."

Many disengaged students view school as an institution that forces them to do work rather than a place to learn, grow, and enjoy. School to them is unsatisfactory—boring and uninteresting. Is it important for students to enjoy school? Yes, it is. Enjoy means "with joy," and we define joy as a feeling of happiness or satisfaction that offers both immediate and long-term gratification. We believe there is a difference between the fun that students have on a roller coaster or video game—that ends when the ride or game is over—and the joy that students feel as they learn and work to reach their potential. When students experience the joy of learning for themselves, they understand the purpose of learning and the value of their education. Our goal is to help disengaged students understand that learning isn't always going to be "roller coaster and video game" fun—but it can result in feelings of satisfaction and success. Your words can spark a student's interest and lead to student enjoyment and engagement in learning.

Many passively disengaged students fall through the cracks, give up, and eventually drop out of school. Often these students are not causing any trouble, so their behaviors are not classified as detrimental to the overall classroom environment. However, they hurt themselves, and their passive behaviors can lead to lifelong negative consequences. Day after day, these students are unaware of the potential they have and the talents they possess. Teachers can make all the difference by helping passively disengaged students see how the day-to-day learning can spark their interests, explore their talents, and help them reach their potential and find success in school and life.

WHAT DO GREAT TEACHERS SAY WHEN...?

A Student is Texting on His Cell Phone or Scrolling through His Computer. (Scenario 4.1)

GTL Reminders to Self:

Remember... Creating engaging and relevant lessons will help keep students tuned in to real-time learning instead of their personal screen time.

Words of Guidance

Remember... By proactively surveying the classroom landscape for the needs of your students and nurturing them when they need it most, you can help prevent passively disengaged students.

Words of Understanding

Remember... Students will make some choices that will disengage them from the lesson, and they will need to be redirected.

Words of Grace

Remember... Technology is here to stay. It can be a helpful tool in the classroom for teaching and learning. It can also be a tool that distracts students from the real-time learning in the moment and negatively impacts their learning and success over time.

Words of Guidance

Remember... Be mindful that you need to demonstrate a balance of love and authority when it comes to technology. Too much love with no authority can lead to no boundaries for students and their personal devices. Too much authority with no love can create a 'lose-lose' situation for both the teacher and the student. In this 'lose-lose' situation, the student could 'lose' the connection and relationship with their teacher, and the teacher could 'lose' the student's willingness to cooperate.

Words of Love

GTL to Share with Students:

"I know you enjoy texting on your phone to your friends. I enjoy texting my friends, too."

Words of Relationship

"But this isn't the right time for that."

Words of Accountability

"It looks like there's something important on your phone. Is everything OK? Remember, if it's not an emergency, we talked about how devices can pull you away from what we're learning in class."

Words of Understanding

"Remember our class expectations about using phones and computers during class? If it's an emergency, please

let me know and you can use it. If it's not an emergency, please put it away so you can get back to our lesson."
Words of Respect

GTL to Use When Talking and Communicating with Parents:

Phone call to discuss appropriate phone and computer use in the classroom.

(A student is consistently texting on his cell phone and scrolling through his computer for personal use which distracts him from the lesson.)

(Note: This GTL phone conversation provides a template you can modify and send to parents as a letter, email, text message, etc.).

"Hello! My name is…. I'm Jamie's teacher. He's not in trouble. Is now a good time for us to talk?"
Words of Respect

"I enjoy having Jamie in my class. He is… (share something personal, positive, and specific that you've experienced with Jamie)."
Words of Encouragement

"I'm calling you to share something that I've noticed a couple of times this week. Jamie has been texting on his phone during class time. First, I asked him if everything was OK and if there was an emergency."
Words of Accountability

"We are teaching students the difference between using their cell phones for classroom lessons or an emergency versus using it for personal texting, video games, or social media. Cell phones can be a great tool for learning in class, but they can also be a huge distraction for students' learning. I'm reaching out to you to make you aware of this issue and let you know that I'm concerned it could impact Jamie's learning."
Words of Guidance

"I wanted to mention this to you and ask you to talk with Jamie about the proper use of a cell phone in our class, so we can have the best learning environment in our classroom for everyone—including Jamie."

            Words of Unity

"Please let me know if you have any questions at all. My hope is for all of our students to feel safe, enjoy school, and learn every day."

            Words of Hope

WHAT DO GREAT TEACHERS SAY WHEN...?

A Student is Sleeping in Class. (Scenario 4.2)

GTL Reminders to Self:

Remember... Take care of the things you can change and be mindful and aware of the things you cannot change.

            Words of Grace

Remember... Take every opportunity to make "one-on-one" connections with students.

            Words of Love

Remember... Sometimes, kids put their head down and sleep in class because they don't understand the lesson or they have something going on at home.

            Words of Understanding

GTL to Share with Students:

(Whispering to student) "I am worried about you sleeping in class. Can you tell me what's going on?"

            Words of Understanding

"I'm concerned about the way you've been sleeping in class... Is everything ok?"

            Words of Love

"I understand that you are feeling sleepy. That must be a difficult way to feel at school. How can I help you? Do you want to talk? Is there anything I can do to help?"
Words of Understanding

GTL to Use When Talking and Communicating with Parents:

Phone call to parent to let them know their child has been sleeping in class.

(Note: This GTL phone conversation provides a template you can modify and send to parents as a letter, email, text message, etc.).

"Hello! My name is …. I'm Jamie's teacher. He's not in trouble. Is now a good time for us to talk?"
Words of Respect

"I enjoy having Jamie in my class. He is… (share something personal, positive, and specific that you've experienced with Jamie)."
Words of Encouragement

"I'm calling you to share something that happened today at school. Jamie seemed extremely tired today. He slept during our morning reading class and then again this afternoon during math class."
Words of Accountability

"I spoke with Jamie in private to find out if he was feeling OK. I wanted to make sure he wasn't sick or needed to go see the school nurse or call home."
Words of Love

"I wanted to mention this to you and work with you on a plan for addressing this sleeping issue so Jamie can have the best learning experience in our classroom."
Words of Unity

"Please let me know if you have any questions at all. My hope is for all of our students to feel safe, enjoy school, and learn every day."
Words of Hope

WHAT DO GREAT TEACHERS SAY WHEN...?

A Student is Not Working On His Assignment and Looks Embarrassed, Troubled, Stressed And/Or Frustrated. (Scenario 4.3)

GTL Reminders to Self:

Remember... When you separate the student from his/her behavior it allows you to 'take a step back' and let the student know 'I still care for you—but I don't like your behavior.'

Words of Grace

Remember... When you show that you care, disengaged students will respond.

Words of Relationship

Remember... Be on the lookout for potential moments when students might feel embarrassed. Embarrassment can lead to shame, confusion, self-consciousness, and disengagement with the lesson.

Words of Guidance

GTL to Share with Students:

(Whispering to student) "It's not fair to the other students—or to you—if you are not working on the assignment that we're all working on."

Words of Accountability

"I am sorry—I didn't realize you were confused and weren't able to complete the assignment. Sometimes, it may take me a while to understand what you are saying or what you need."

Words of Grace

"I noticed you looked stressed. How can I help you?"

Words of Love

"You look troubled. Let's talk about what's troubling you today, and we can decide how to work through this problem together so it won't trouble you tomorrow."

Words of Hope

"Whenever learning becomes difficult for you, don't allow yourself to feel stupid or embarrassed, because then you might become discouraged and give up. It is my job to help you avoid those feelings by answering all of your questions and teaching you how to learn new information."

Words of Encouragement

WHAT DO GREAT TEACHERS SAY WHEN...?

A Student is Not Paying Attention to the Lesson and is Daydreaming in Class. (Scenario 4.4)

GTL Reminders to Self:

Remember... Whenever it is possible, try to get to know your students. Talk to them and get to know what they like or dislike. Try to find out what their passions are and what they really care about.

Words of Relationship

Remember... Students' perceptions guide their feelings, and to truly understand their feelings, we have to acknowledge those perceptions.

Words of Understanding

Remember... Sometimes, kids don't pay attention and daydream because they don't understand the lesson or they have something going on at home or they're bored.

Words of Understanding

GTL to Share with Students:

"It looks like you have a problem concentrating today. How can I help you focus on your work?"
Words of Accountability

"You don't seem like yourself today. I have noticed that you are having trouble paying attention and might need my help. Let's talk after class."
Words of Love

"When you're starting to get confused and tune out from our lesson— just ask me for help."
Words of Guidance

(Whispering to student) "I know this assignment is confusing right now, but remember it's so important to pay attention to our lesson. When it clicks for you and you finally understand how to do it, you'll feel really good about it."
Words of Encouragement

WHAT DO GREAT TEACHERS SAY WHEN...?

A Student Never Verbally Participates in Class. (Scenario 4.5)

GTL Reminders to Self:

Remember... Disengaged students often blend in and choose not to participate. See them as potential contributors and encourage them to be an active participant in your classroom.
Words of Hope

Remember... A classroom filled with hope brings energy to the students and the teacher.
Words of Hope

Remember... Sometimes, kids don't participate because they're shy, introverted, or afraid to speak out.

Words of Understanding

Remember... Sometimes, kids don't participate because they can't read or they have a speech impairment. This awareness could be an opportunity to connect these students with the special services they need to be successful.

Words of Understanding

GTL to Share with Students:

(To the whole class) "I know you might be afraid to speak out in class, but I promise that we want to hear what you have to say, what you believe, and the questions you have."

Words of Encouragement

"I understand if you don't feel like talking about it right now—just know I'm available to listen when you feel like it."

Words of Understanding

(To the whole class) "This lesson is going to be great! It's something we all need to know, so I'll be expecting everyone's participation."

Words of High Expectations

"I can see you one day: running your own business, being a fireman, teaching students in your own classroom, being a nurse in a hospital or whatever you want to be."

Words of Hope

"I care about you and want you to be successful. Help me understand what I can do to help you get involved in our classroom discussions?"

Words of Understanding

(To the whole class) "In our classroom, we want to establish a climate where no one feels embarrassed to share. We will work together to respect each other's opinions and thoughts."
Words of Respect

"Don't be afraid to share your story with the class. We want to hear what you have to say. I know you can do this."
Words of High Expectations

WHAT DO GREAT TEACHERS SAY WHEN...?

A Passively Disengaged Student Has Failing Grades in Your Class. (Scenario 4.6)

GTL Reminders to Self:

Remember... Sometimes, students disengage because of a fear of failure.
Words of Understanding

Remember... Sometimes, students have failing grades because they do not see how the lesson relates to them and their world.
Words of Relationship

Remember... Sometimes, students have failing grades because they're 'shy, introverted, or afraid to speak out,' which can cause them to slip through the cracks.
Words of Understanding

Remember... Sometimes, students have failing grades because they can't read.
Words of Understanding

Remember... When students are disappointed about their failing grade on an assignment, encourage them

not to give up. Consider helping them create a plan to redo the assignment.
Words of Encouragement

Remember… Students can have failing grades because of academic issues, social issues, behavior issues, homework issues, apathy issues and/or lack of interest.
Words of Understanding

GTL to Share with Students:

"I want to help you in any way possible—I'll spend extra time with you to work on your math/reading."
Words of Guidance

(Whispering to student) "You've almost got it. I know this isn't "roller coaster or video game" fun, but when you finish this project, you'll feel great!"
Words of Encouragement

"I am excited to see that you are enjoying the activity today and working hard to complete your part of it. I knew you could do it!"
Words of High Expectations

"Let's look at how this lesson is impacting your world today and how it relates to you, your family, and your community."
Words of Relationship

"I can tell you're really disappointed about your test grade, and you might want to give up. Let's make a plan together so you can succeed next time."
Words of Encouragement

"It looks like you need a chance to redo this assignment. I know you can do better than this, and I want to help you get there."
Words of Grace

"Don't keep being hard on yourself about your past grades. Let's put those behind us and move ahead!"

Words of Grace

"When you have tried your very best at something and it still doesn't seem good enough—don't give up and stop trying. We'll keep working together to figure it out."

Words of Unity

"I know that you are still struggling with your reading, but every day you are working harder and harder and you are improving. We will continue to work together, and I believe that by the end of the year, you will be caught up with the skills you need to be successful next year."

Words of Encouragement

GTL to Use When Talking and Communicating with Parents:

Phone call to parent to discuss child's failing grades, share our concerns, and work together to create a support plan for their child both at school and at home.

(Note: This GTL phone conversation provides a template you can modify and send to parents as a letter, email, text message, etc.).

"Hello! My name is …. I'm Jamie's teacher. He's not in trouble. Is now a good time for us to talk?"

Words of Respect

"I enjoy having Jamie in my class. He is…(share something personal, positive, and specific that you've experienced with Jamie)."

Words of Encouragement

"I wanted to call and share an update on how Jamie is doing in class."

Words of Relationship

"Jamie is having trouble with some of the work that we're doing, and I'm concerned about him. If you remember, you and I talked at our Open House about how Jamie would be bringing home his Weekly Folder with his work and graded papers. In the folder Jamie is bringing home today, he has some failing grades, and I wanted you to know about it before he brought them home."

Words of Accountability

"I've been talking to Jamie and working with him individually, and I also need your insight and influence and help. Could we meet sometime this week and sit down together to design a plan for Jamie? Together, we can get him the support he needs to be successful."

Words of Unity

"When would be a good time for you to meet?"

Words of Respect

"I'm looking forward to meeting with you and working together for Jamie. He has plenty of time to catch up and get back on track."

Words of Hope

"Please let me know if you have any questions at all. My hope is for all of our students to feel safe, enjoy school, and learn every day."

Words of Hope

GTL Classroom Activities to Transform Student Behavior and Your Classroom Culture

GTL Classroom Activities for Passively Disengaged Students

We see these activities as either "in the moment" or a time to circle up for classroom meetings to encourage student voice and student engagement in your classroom. We see the teacher as a facilitator and co-learner during these GTL activities and students as active participants in learning how to "see the classroom through the lens of the teacher" and how to manage their own behavior.

1. (Role-Play GTL Scenario for students who are passively not paying attention.) Select one student to role-play a teacher and one student to role-play a student who is passively not paying attention in class. Allow time for the role-playing teacher to try to engage the disengaged student. After the role-play, ask the passively disengaged student if what the role-playing teacher said was helpful. Encourage the other students in the class to help the role-playing teacher with what to say and how to respectfully respond to the passively disengaged student so they will start to pay attention. Conclude the role-playing activity with a discussion of how you, as the teacher, can respectfully engage passively disengaged students in your classroom.
2. (Hit the Pause Button for Discussion on Classroom Distractions when you see multiple students passively disengaged in the lesson: distracted by their devices, daydreaming, sleeping, etc.). Share with the students that you are going to "Hit the Pause Button" on the lesson and take important time to discuss classroom distractions and how to deal with them and prevent them. Ask students to think about the things that distract them the most from learning and divide their attention in the classroom. Allow time for each student to share one of their distractions and list them on the board. Discuss how to "tune out" distractions during class time and "tune in" to learning with their undivided attention. Conclude the discussion by sharing how you personally "tune out" distractions.
3. (Revisiting the Classroom Rules and Behavior Expectations about "Proper Cell Phone/Computer Use in the Classroom.") Remind the students about "Our Classroom Rules and Behavior Expectations" that everyone helped create and agreed to follow. Spend time discussing the rule

about proper cell phone and computer use. Share with students the difference between using their cell phones for classroom lessons or an emergency versus using them for personal texting, video games, or social media. Talk about how cell phones can be a great tool for learning in class but how they can also be a huge distraction for their learning. Conclude the discussion by reassuring the students that using the phone for an emergency is fine and to please let you know if there is an emergency.

5

What Do Great Teachers Say When a Student is an Attention Seeker?

What do you say when a student is disrupting class and is constantly wanting to be seen and/or heard (e.g., Class Entertainer, Social Butterfly, Excessive Talker, and Tattle Tale). This chapter provides teacher-friendly charts with Great Teacher Language (GTL) Reminders to Self, GTL to Share with Students, GTL to Use When Talking and Communicating with Parents, and GTL Classroom Activities specifically related to the following:

Scenario 5.1: A student is constantly raising his/her hand and saying, "Teacher, Teacher…".
Scenario 5.2: A student is up out of his/her seat, socializing with other students, throwing away trash, sharpening his/her pencil, and so on.
Scenario 5.3: A student says, "Teacher, he's bothering me!"
Scenario 5.4: A student is being the class entertainer.
Scenario 5.5: A student is always raising his/her hand, wanting to answer every question or is constantly asking questions.
Scenario 5.6: A student is always talking in class.

> We know these are not the only attention-seeking behaviors that happen in your classroom. These specific scenarios are a starting point for you to develop your Great Teacher Language (GTL) for your classroom. For some of our student behavior scenarios, we have included GTL examples for you to use when talking with parents. These GTL examples are templates for phone conversations, emails, or other types of messages to develop strong communication between teachers and parents and to promote understanding, relationships, trust, and collaboration.

Every student in your classroom needs attention. Some of them need assistance with academic problems; others need help with social problems. The greatest attention seekers in your classroom are relentless in their pursuit. They seem to want attention from everyone, all the time. Many of these students find great pleasure in socializing at school. They talk excessively or try to entertain their classmates throughout the day. Others try to gain attention by policing the class and telling the teacher everything that's done wrong. Their behaviors are not usually malicious; however, they are not learning, they often annoy other students, and they disrupt class and impede learning. Your Language of Practice (LoP) in the form of GTL can offer these attention-seeking students the accountability, encouragement, grace, guidance, high expectations, hope, love, relationships, respect, understanding, and unity they need and provide redirection for their actions. Your words and actions will show their classmates how to relate and respond to these attention seekers.

Let's face it. Sometimes, students who need extra attention can be challenging. Why do some students need more attention than others? Giving appropriate attention to any student in your classroom starts with separating the student from their behavior. With attention seekers, we must look beyond the aggravation and share an attitude of grace, love, understanding, and accountability which conveys, "You are worth my time and undivided attention, I want to understand what you need, but right now is not the time for us to talk." These students need accountability for their behavior, and they also need your individual attention and some quality time. They need to know that you care. They need your eye contact, and they need to know that you are listening to them. Your actions and words demonstrate to them that you are interested in who they are, what they are doing, and what they need.

Many of the discipline issues in the classroom can be addressed with quality time. Yet we often feel like there aren't enough hours in the day to pay attention to each student individually. However, when we spend just a few minutes of quality time listening attentively to a student, it can fill their need for attention and give us insight into how we can redirect their misbehavior.

Sometimes, an insatiable appetite for attention prevents attention seekers from seeing the detrimental effects of their behavior. Class entertainers display silly and immature behaviors. Social butterflies often distract and annoy other students. Without the proper guidance and accountability, these misbehaviors can have negative long-term consequences. Our job is to help attention seekers minimize their extreme need for attention and replace it with an increased self-awareness and personal accountability.

Attention seekers are seeking affirmation from others. Class entertainers want laughs, while social butterflies want to "know and be known." To satisfy their appetite for attention, teachers can help these students channel their energies into more-productive efforts. For example, class entertainers can get laughs and applause performing in the school play. Social butterflies can network in school clubs and other extracurricular activities. Our language can provide the guidance and direction that these students need to encourage and ensure their success.

We can promote unity and teamwork in our classroom by modeling to all students that everyone deserves our respect. If teachers are not careful, our words and actions can demonstrate to students that we don't like the attention seekers. Our goal is for students to learn, and the attention seekers can often deter learning. The way we talk about attention seekers and the way we talk to them show how we feel about them. Students can misinterpret our words and actions. If students think our words and actions indicate a certain dislike for a student, the other students may feel they have the right to feel and act the same. It is so important to carefully deal with attention-seekers while maintaining the unity within our classroom.

What do you say to help guide attention seekers from socially unacceptable behaviors to socially acceptable behaviors in the classroom? How will you meet their needs and/or provide a setting where their needs can be met? When we hold students accountable for inappropriate behavior while maintaining their dignity, students observe grace in action. It helps them understand that inappropriate behavior does not dictate whether or not we show someone respect.

WHAT DO GREAT TEACHERS SAY WHEN...?

A Student is Constantly Raising His/Her Hand and Saying, "Teacher, Teacher..." (Scenario 5.1)

GTL Reminders to Self:

Remember... It might seem easier in the short term to give in to students and let them have their way, but they desperately need structured accountability and someone to hold them accountable for their actions.

Words of Accountability

Remember... When you harbor feelings of resentment and frustration, it can impact your ability to see the students' real needs.

Words of Grace

Remember... Classroom experiences can be some of the most influential experiences of a student's life—make sure those experiences are positive and uplifting for all students!

Words of Hope

GTL to Share with Students:

"Wait a second. Let me stop what I'm doing because I really want to listen to you."

Words of Love

"This just isn't the time for this right now, but I am really interested in what you need to share with me. As soon as I am finished with this activity, we will talk."
Words of Relationship

"I am sorry—I didn't realize you had a problem. Sometimes, it may take me a while to understand what you are wanting to say or what you need."
Words of Understanding

WHAT DO GREAT TEACHERS SAY WHEN...?

A Student is Up Out of His/Her Seat, Socializing with Other Students, Throwing Away Trash, Sharpening His/Her Pencil. (Scenario 5.2)

GTL Reminders to Self:

Remember... Don't forget to call parents when things are going well. They would love to get a positive phone call concerning their child!
Words of Encouragement

Remember... When we allow the same misbehavior to go on and on without accountability, we send the unintentional message that we do not expect the students to meet the guidelines and high expectations for our classroom.
Words of Accountability

Remember... Rather than harboring ill feelings for misbehaving students like the social butterfly, grant them grace and dig deep to get at the root of the problem.
Words of Grace

Remember... There might be times when your students are off task and distracting others from learning. This behavior may be a signal that they need extra attention for instructional or emotional reasons. When you give them extra attention, you are showing them they are important to you.
Words of Understanding

Remember... Students need to have an outlet, so allow them opportunities to talk and socialize throughout the day.

Words of Understanding

GTL to Share with Students:

(Sharing with the whole class) "If you are out of your seat and distracting other students, I promise I won't single you out or raise my voice. I will quietly and respectfully make eye contact with you, tap you on the shoulder, and remind you to go to your seat."

Words of Respect

"If you have something you would like to share with someone else, please wait until we finish the lesson and then you will have the opportunity to discuss what you have to say."

Words of Guidance

"When you're out of your seat, it disrupts the lesson. You're not learning, and it keeps the other students from learning, too."

Words of Accountability

(Talking to student alone) "I'm concerned about what you have been doing in your other classes. I hear you are up out of your seat, talking all the time, and disrupting class. You can do better than that—I know you can. We've all seen the amazing changes you've made in our class!"

Words of High Expectations

"I noticed you stayed in your seat for the whole math lesson today. When you decide to follow our rules, you set a great example for the other students to follow."

Words of Encouragement

WHAT DO GREAT TEACHERS SAY WHEN...?

A Student Says, "Teacher, He's Bothering Me!" (Scenario 5.3)

GTL Reminders to Self:

Remember... Teach your students the difference between tattling and reporting. Tattling is saying something to the teacher to gain attention or just to get someone else in trouble. Reporting is sharing information with the teacher that helps the student, keeps trouble from happening, or helps someone else. The goal of reporting is to maintain a safe classroom environment for all students.

Words of Guidance

Remember... Encourage tattle tales to confront specific situations by offering them the words to use to convey their feelings and thoughts to the right person.

Words of Encouragement

Remember... Really try to get to know every one of your students and why they act the way they do.

Words of Relationship

Remember... Some students need to be taught how to interact with others. We can rehearse, role-play, and model good behavior and discuss the issue together.

Words of Guidance

GTL to Share with Students:

"Let me stop what I'm doing because I want to listen to you and find out what's really happening with you and the other student."

Words of Understanding

"If you are just trying to get someone in trouble, you need to rethink what you want to tell me."

Words of Guidance

"When someone is bothering you, you should confidently and politely ask that person to stop. If he doesn't stop, let me know."
Words of Guidance

(Talking privately to both students) "Jamie, I appreciate you respectfully sharing your frustrations with me. Let's talk about how each of you sees this situation. I want to hear from both of you about what's going on."
Words of Understanding

"If you have a problem with any of your classmates, make it known as soon as possible. Let's address our concerns openly, honestly, and respectfully, so we don't hold grudges."
Words of Grace

"Remember, before you choose to pick on someone, ask yourself, 'How would I feel if someone picked on me?'"
Words of Guidance

GTL to use when talking and communicating with parents:

Proactive phone call to encourage parent and celebrate student behavior.

(A student is learning how to stand up for himself and understand the difference between tattling and reporting, and you share an update with their parent.)

(Note: This GTL phone conversation provides a template you can modify and send to parents as a letter, email, text message, etc.).

"Hello! My name is …. I'm Jamie's teacher. He's not in trouble. Is now a good time for us to talk?"
Words of Respect

"I enjoy having Jamie in my class. He is… (share something personal, positive, and specific that you've experienced with Jamie)."
Words of Encouragement

"I'm calling you to share something that happened today at school. Jamie and another student were having an issue in class, and Jamie came to me to share the student was bothering him."

Words of Accountability

"We are teaching students the difference between tattling and reporting. Tattling is saying something to the teacher to gain attention or just to get someone else in trouble. Reporting is sharing information with the teacher that helps the student, keeps trouble from happening, or helps someone else. The goal of reporting is to maintain a safe classroom environment for all students."

Words of Guidance

"I was really proud of the way Jamie handled the situation. He respectfully asked the student to stop, and I talked with both students to get to the bottom of the issue."

Words of Encouragement

"Please let me know if you have any questions at all. My hope is for all of our students to feel safe, enjoy school, and learn every day."

Words of Hope

WHAT DO GREAT TEACHERS SAY WHEN...?

A Student is Being the Class Entertainer. (Scenario 5.4)

GTL Reminders to Self:

Remember... There is a reason why students act the way they do, so find out what's going on and what is driving those behaviors.

Words of Understanding

Remember... All students are so different and so interesting in their own way. Some of them are outgoing, and some of them are quiet. Find ways to get to know each student better. You can learn a lot from their differences.

Words of Understanding

Remember... Rather than harboring ill feelings for misbehaving students like the class entertainer, grant them grace and dig deep to get at the root of the problem.

Words of Grace

GTL to Share with Students:

"You are not in trouble, but we need to have a heart-to-heart conversation about your behavior."

Words of Accountability

"There's a time for work and a time for play."

Words of Guidance

"You really need to try out for the school play—you would be great!"

Words of Encouragement

GTL to use when talking and communicating with parents:

Phone call to promote unity with parent.

(The student is continually trying to make people laugh which warrants a call to their parent.)

(Note: This GTL phone conversation provides a template you can modify and send to parents as a letter, email, text message, etc.).

"Hello! My name is ... I'm Jamie's teacher. He's not in trouble. Is now a good time for us to talk?"

Words of Respect

"I enjoy having Jamie in my class. He is... (share something personal, positive, and specific that you've experienced with Jamie)."

Words of Encouragement

What Do Great Teachers Say When a Student is an Attention Seeker? ◆ 85

"I'm calling you to share something that's been happening at school. Jamie has a terrific personality and is liked by his classmates. He has been trying to make students laugh in class, and it causes disruptions in their learning, and his own learning has suffered."
Words of Accountability

"I wanted to mention this to you and work with you on a plan for addressing these issues, so we can have the best learning environment in the classroom for everyone—including Jamie."
Words of Unity

"Please let me know if you have any questions at all. My hope is for all of our students to feel safe, enjoy school, and learn every day."
Words of Hope

WHAT DO GREAT TEACHERS SAY WHEN...?

A Student is Always Raising His/Her Hand, Wanting to Answer Every Question or is Constantly Asking Questions. (Scenario 5.5)

GTL Reminders to Self:

Remember... The questions students ask can provide tremendous insight into how much they trust you—and how safe they feel in your classroom.
Words of Relationship

Remember... Sometimes, using 'you' messages can place blame whereas using 'I' messages can be a softer way of expressing your emotions while holding the student accountable.
Words of Accountability

Remember... One way some students learn is by asking questions. Their questions can help them, and the other students, understand the lesson better. However, sometimes, students' questions are irrelevant, unnecessary, or not on topic or are for attention. These students need guidance in how to ask acceptable questions.

Words of Understanding

Remember… When students feel free to ask questions, it provides a classroom environment that fosters creativity and learning.

Words of Relationship

GTL to Share with Students:

(Talking privately with the student) "You're not in trouble, but we need to have a heart-to-heart conversation about how important it is to let other students have an opportunity to answer questions and feel successful."

Words of Accountability

"I want to hear what you have to ask, I am interested in your questions, so jot those questions down on a post-it note and put them on our Parking Lot board for later."

Words of Guidance

"Your questions, right now, are not about our lesson. I'm glad you're interested in asking questions. If you would focus your questions on our classwork, you would help us all!"

Words of Hope

"I noticed you let other students answer questions today. What a great example for other students to follow."

Words of Encouragement

(Whispering to student) "I appreciate how you waited to raise your hand and gave the other students your attention while they were speaking. This is an act of respect for others."

Words of Respect

WHAT DO GREAT TEACHERS SAY WHEN...?

A Student is Always Talking in Class. (Scenario 5.6)

GTL Reminders to Self:

Remember... There are going to be days that you don't like what your students do, such as constant talking, but they still need you to love them and hold them accountable for those actions.

Words of Love

Remember... Rather than harboring ill feelings for misbehaving students like the constant talker, grant them grace and dig deep to get at the root of the problem.

Words of Grace

Remember... There might be times when your students are talking and distracting others from learning. This behavior may be a signal that they need extra attention for instructional or emotional reasons. When you give them that extra attention, you are showing them they are important to you.

Words of Understanding

Remember... Students need to have an outlet, so allow them opportunities to talk and socialize throughout the day.

Words of Understanding

GTL to Share with Students:

(Whispering to a student) "I've noticed you're talking too much while I'm teaching, but I'm going to be patient and give you another chance, so we can figure out the best times to talk."

Words of Grace

"We are going to learn by talking and by listening, so we are going to have to help each other understand when it's time to talk and when it's time to listen."

Words of Unity

"I was so glad to see how you acted in our assembly today. You showed that you know how to pay attention and be a role model for other students. I'm excited to see you do the same thing in our classroom."
Words of High Expectations

GTL to use when talking and communicating with parents:

Phone call to discuss student accountability with parent.

(The student is continually talking during class which warrants a call to his parent.)

(Note: This GTL phone conversation provides a template you can modify and send to parents as a letter, email, text message, etc.).

"Hello! My name is …. I'm Jamie's teacher. He's not in trouble. Is now a good time for us to talk?"
Words of Respect

"I enjoy having Jamie in my class. He is… (share something personal, positive, and specific that you've experienced with Jamie)."
Words of Encouragement

"I'm calling you to share something that we've been discussing in class. We are teaching the students the importance of when to talk and when to listen. We have lots of times throughout the day when students have time to talk and other times when they need to listen. Jamie is having a tough time listening when other people are talking. He's constantly talking in class, and it causes disruptions in their learning, and his own learning has suffered."
Words of Accountability

"I wanted to mention this to you and ask you to talk with Jamie about the importance of listening in our class, so we can have the best learning environment in our classroom for everyone—including Jamie."
Words of Unity

> "Please let me know if you have any questions at all. My hope is for all of our students to feel safe, enjoy school, and learn every day."
>
> Words of Hope

GTL Classroom Activities to Transform Student Behavior and Your Classroom Culture

GTL Classroom Activities for Attention Seekers

We see these activities as either "in the moment" or a time to circle up for classroom meetings to encourage student voice and student engagement in your classroom. We see the teacher as a facilitator and co-learner during these GTL activities and students as active participants in learning how to "see the classroom through the lens of the teacher" and how to manage their own behavior.

1. (Role-Play GTL Scenario for "Difference between Tattling and Reporting.") Select one student to role-play a teacher and two other students to role-play two students (one student will demonstrate tattling, and the other student will demonstrate reporting). The first student (tattling) says, "Jamie is looking at me funny. He's also not doing his work and chewing gum and not paying attention." The second student (reporting) says, "I saw Jamie hit Sarah on the playground, and she is out there crying." Encourage the other students in the class to vote on which student is tattling and which student is reporting. Continue with more student volunteers to demonstrate tattling and reporting.
2. (Hit the Pause Button for Class Discussion on "When to Talk and When to Listen.")

    Share with the students that you are going to "Hit the Pause Button" on the lesson and take important time to discuss When to Talk and When to Listen. The teacher will write When to Talk and When to Listen on the whiteboard.

Ask the whole class for their personal answers for When to Talk and When to Listen. Students can use post-it notes or share their responses with the teacher. Compile all the responses to refer to later. Conclude the discussion by reminding students they have lots of time throughout the day to talk and sharing your personal reasons for When to Talk and When to Listen.

3. (Revisiting the Classroom Rules and Behavior Expectations about "Being Respectful to Others") Remind the students about "Our Classroom Rules and Behavior Expectations" that everyone helped create and agreed to follow. Spend time discussing the classroom expectation of being respectful to others. Discuss some disruptive behaviors like getting out of your seat and talking to students, throwing away trash during the lesson, talking when the teacher is talking, or trying to make other people laugh, and explain how these behaviors cause distractions and are disrespectful to the teacher and other students. Remind the students it is their responsibility to follow these student-and-teacher expectations to practice self-management and encourage the best possible learning environment for everyone.

6

What Do Great Teachers Say When a Student Outburst Happens?

What do you say when you want to appropriately and respectfully address an inappropriate outburst in your classroom? This chapter provides teacher-friendly charts with Great Teacher Language (GTL) Reminders to Self, GTL to Share with Students, GTL to Use When Talking and Communicating with Parents, and GTL Classroom Activities specifically related to the following:

Scenario 6.1: A student yells out, "This is so boring!"
Scenario 6.2: A student yells out, "This is stupid. I can't do it!"
Scenario 6.3: A student yells out, "Why do we need to learn this?"
Scenario 6.4: A student yells out profanity, "@#$%"
Scenario 6.5: A student yells out a verbally aggressive outburst and/or acts out a physically aggressive outburst.

We know these are not the only outbursts that happen in your classroom. These specific scenarios are a starting point for you to develop your Great Teacher Language (GTL) for your classroom. For some of our student behavior scenarios, we have included GTL examples for you to use when talking with parents. These GTL examples are templates for phone

> conversations, emails, or other types of messages to develop strong communication between teachers and parents and to promote understanding, relationships, trust, and collaboration.

Wanted: Uninterrupted quality time for teaching and learning. No intercom, no knocks on the door, and no student outbursts. Instructional time without distractions is a teacher's dream. It is easy to become frustrated when distractions occur. However, we need to be careful in how we deal with distractions, especially inappropriate student outbursts, because they affect everyone and can lead to larger problems. We must model appropriate responses to outbursts that respect the student, quietly redirect the student, diffuse the situation, and minimize the loss of instructional time. Your Language of Practice (LoP) in the form of GTL can offer these disruptive students the accountability, encouragement, grace, guidance, high expectations, hope, love, relationships, respect, understanding, and unity they need in the moment and beyond.

An inappropriate outburst is like a sign around a student's neck that says, "I need your help." Such behavior is a loud and clear indication that the student is feeling upset by something, and it might indicate a deeper emotional issue they are experiencing. The sooner we can get to the bottom of what is troubling the student, the sooner the student can reengage with learning. Student outbursts in the classroom can range from shouting out answers to loud disrespectful profanity or verbally aggressive and/or physically aggressive outbursts. Whatever the case, we must try to uncover the reason for these behaviors and address them with care. Some inappropriate student outbursts can be addressed in the classroom, while other outburst behaviors may require more support from the teacher, guidance counselors, or parents for a long-term solution.

When student outbursts occur in the classroom, there is a tendency for us to give back to students what they give us. If they get loud, we get loud. If they get loud *and* angry, then we get loud *and* angry. It is difficult not to react with a loud voice when students are loud and even more difficult not to show anger when students are angry. An inappropriate student outburst affects everyone, and your response to it will also affect everyone. Every student in the classroom anxiously waits to see how you are going to handle the situation. They all need to see and hear us maintain the dignity of the student while we hold them accountable for their actions.

Inappropriate student outbursts demonstrate a lack of self-management. Students need us to model grace, self-management, and self-respect with our words and actions. They need to see us respond to stressful situations with poise and understanding.

WHAT DO GREAT TEACHERS SAY WHEN...?

A Student Yells Out, "This is So Boring!" (Scenario 6.1)

GTL Reminders to Self:

Remember... Make sure the students understand that if they disrupt class, the primary focus is on the learning that day, so try very hard not to personalize every disruption, to keep the focus on the learning, and to let the students know how important it is that we make progress every day.

Words of High Expectations

Remember... If a student is disrupting instruction, try to continue your teaching. In order to maintain the dignity of the student and hold him/her accountable, walk over and whisper to the student that you will discuss his/her behavior after class.

Words of Relationship

Remember... No student is perfect. All of them make mistakes. Outbursts can indicate a deeper issue. Be sure to give them a second chance whenever possible while letting them know their behavior was not acceptable.

Words of Grace

Remember... Eliminating boredom in the classroom is the responsibility of both the student and the teacher.

Words of Accountability

GTL to Share with Students:

(Whispering to student) "In our classroom, we don't act this way. I understand that something may have caused you to act that way, but you will need to choose a different way to act instead. What do you think you could have said instead? How could you have acted differently?"

Words of Accountability

(Whispering to student) "I don't want to single you out in front of everybody, but we need to talk after class about your behavior just now."

Words of Respect

"Help me understand why you said that."

Words of Understanding

(Talking individually to the student) "Talk to me about why you think this is so boring. I really want to know what you are thinking and how I can make it more interesting."

Words of Understanding

WHAT DO GREAT TEACHERS SAY WHEN...?

A Student Yells Out, "This is Stupid, I Can't Do It!" (Scenario 6.2)

GTL Reminders to Self:

Remember... Sometimes, kids act out because they don't understand the work.

Words of Encouragement

Remember... When you start to get frustrated, slow down, breathe, and take a few minutes to calm down. You don't want to say or do something to harm your relationship with your students.

Words of Relationship

Remember...When dealing with any discipline problem, it is essential to get to the root of the problem.

Words of Understanding

GTL to Share with Students:

"Yesterday you looked like you understood this, but today you're obviously confused and frustrated. Let's go back over what we did yesterday in class to see what you don't understand, so you don't get to the point where you shout out in class."

Words of Understanding

"When you find yourself having a hard time, rather than speaking out in class, let's come up with a signal that you can show me so we can talk together and meet to solve the problem."

Words of Love

"I know it gets frustrating—but you've almost got it—you're almost there—just hang in there for a little while longer."

Words of Hope

WHAT DO GREAT TEACHERS SAY WHEN...?

A Student Yells, "Why Do We Have To Learn This?" (Scenario 6.3)

GTL Reminders to Self:

Remember... There are going to be days when you don't like what your students say, but they still need you to love them and hold them accountable for those inappropriate outbursts.

Words of Grace

Remember... Many inappropriate outbursts can be prevented by proactively surveying the classroom

landscape for the needs of your students and nurturing them when they need it the most.
Words of Grace

Remember... Helping students understand 'The Why' of what they are learning is essential.
Words of Understanding

Remember... Helping students learn how to ask questions respectfully can promote trust, foster relationships, and optimize learning.
Words of Relationship

GTL to Share with Students:

"I can tell that you are frustrated about today's work—let me explain why this assignment is important and how you can use it in your life."
Words of Guidance

(Whispering to student) "In the future, it would be better for you to share your frustrations with me privately and respectfully—like I'm doing right now. You can always share your frustrations about our classwork with me."
Words of Respect

(Sharing with the whole class) "Outbursts are not OK, and they disrupt our class lessons. However, I appreciate how you asked, 'Why is this work important?' Next time, please feel free to ask me that question, in private."
Words of Accountability

(Whispering to student) "Help me understand why you think this work is stupid? Tell me more. Is it too hard? Is it boring? I want to understand."
Words of Understanding

WHAT DO GREAT TEACHERS SAY WHEN...?

A Student Yells Out Profanity. (Scenario 6.4)

GTL Reminders to Self:

Remember... Singling students out when they've demonstrated disrespect (e.g., an inappropriate outburst) can cause additional shame and can escalate the problem. So, respectfully ask the student to step outside in the hall to discuss the issue.

Words of Respect

Remember... When you separate the student from his/her behavior, it allows you to 'take a step back' and let the student know that 'I still care for you—but I don't like your behavior.'

Words of Grace

Remember... Don't allow disrespectful student behavior to become a personal conflict: you vs. student. Keep the focus on helping the student and not on defending yourself, maintaining your power, saving face, and so on.

Words of Unity

GTL to Share with Students:

"Your yelling out in class really took me by surprise—what's going on?"

Words of Understanding

"You know, we just don't talk that way in our classroom. I know that something may have caused you to act that way, but you need to stop using that language. What do you think you could have said instead?"

Words of Accountability

"That is not appropriate language. That is not how we all agreed to talk in our classroom."

Words of Unity

"If you find yourself having a moment when you really want to say something that you shouldn't—stop—think of all of the other possibilities—and choose your words carefully."

Words of Guidance

GTL to Use When Talking and Communicating with Parents:

A student's use of profanity warrants a call to parent.

(Note: This GTL phone conversation provides a template you can modify and send to parents as a letter, email, text message, etc.).

"Hello! My name is …. I'm Jamie's teacher. Is now a good time for us to talk?"

Words of Respect

"I'm calling you to share something that happened at school today. Jamie yelled out profanity and disrupted class."

Words of Accountability

"I have talked with Jamie to get an understanding of his behavior. I asked Jamie to help me understand why he used that type of language. I asked him if he was frustrated or angry or didn't feel well. He didn't really want to talk with me about it today."

Words of Understanding

"So, I wanted to reach out and make you aware of his behavior and work together to get to the bottom of what is going on with Jamie."

Words of Understanding

"We have school policies to make sure our school is a safe place for everyone, and the school's policy is clear about profanity. (State your school's policy for this type of behavior.)"

Words of Accountability

"Before we finish our conversation, I wanted to share that I have enjoyed having Jamie in my class. He is… (share something personal, positive, and specific that you've experienced with Jamie)."
Words of Encouragement

"At the beginning of the school year at the parent Open House, we talked about the importance of maintaining a strong relationship and open communication between home and school."
Words of Relationship

"Please let me know if you have any questions at all. My hope is for all of our students to feel safe, enjoy school, and learn every day."
Words of Hope

WHAT DO GREAT TEACHERS SAY WHEN…?

A Student Yells Out a Verbally Aggressive Outburst and/or Acts Out a Physically Aggressive Outburst. (Scenario 6.5)

(This scenario is a serious one. Anytime students are verbally aggressive or physically aggressive in your classroom, it is a chaotic, scary, and emotionally and physically charged experience for you and all the students in the classroom. Whether they throw a chair, fall to the floor screaming, or act out more intense or aggressive behaviors—it's physically and emotionally stressful for everyone. Notify your school principal immediately to help you handle the situation. Hopefully, these GTL examples offer guidance and understanding for you during this very stressful experience.)

GTL Reminders to Self:

Remember… Aggressive outbursts can indicate a deeper emotional or physical issue. Be sure to give students a second chance whenever possible while letting them know their behavior was not acceptable.

Words of Grace

Remember… When you're setting up your classroom rules and behavior expectations, it's important for you to make all students aware of the consequences for aggressive outbursts in your classroom before they happen.

Words of Guidance

Remember… Rather than harboring ill feelings for a student who made an aggressive outburst in your classroom, demonstrate grace and dig deep to get to the root of the problem.

Words of Grace

Remember… In some cases of aggressive outbursts, you alone may not be able to solve a student's problem, and you will need the help of the guidance counselor and other support personnel.

Words of Guidance

Remember… Wanting to get to the root of the problem when dealing with aggressive outbursts is a sign of love and care.

Words of Love

Remember… Provide students a list of effective strategies they can use to prevent aggressive outbursts before they happen (e.g., go to the teacher immediately to ask for help, go to a safe place in the classroom and try to settle down, put your head down on your desk and count to 10, or ask to talk with the guidance counselor).

Words of Guidance

GTL to Share with Students:

(Speaking individually with the outburst student) "In our classroom, we don't act this way. I understand that something may have caused you to act that way, but you cannot act that way in our classroom."

Words of Accountability

(After the incident is over) "Help me understand how you were feeling just now. Were you angry at me or someone?"

Words of Understanding

"That's unacceptable classroom behavior, so I think it would be best if you went to the safe place in our classroom and tried to settle down. After you have calmed down, let's talk about what happened."

Words of Accountability

(After the phone call with parents) "I appreciate your being honest with your parents about what happened—that's the first step in getting to the truth of what caused you to act that way. Once we know what caused it, we can learn how to prevent it from happening again."

Words of Encouragement

(To the whole class) "Thank you for staying calm and for helping me with this situation. Please stay in your seats and work quietly while I call the principal."

Words of Guidance

(To the whole class) "When you are feeling upset or angry and want to act out—stop—and think about what you can do instead. You can come to me immediately and we can talk, you can go to the safe place in the classroom to settle down, you can put your head

down and count to 10, or you can ask to go and talk with the guidance counselor."
Words of Guidance

"I'm glad we worked together on this plan for improving your behavior. I know it's going to work because you are a very determined person, and when you give your attention to something, you get it done!"
Words of Encouragement

GTL to Use When Talking and Communicating with Parents:

Phone call to discuss a student's behavior in the classroom: A student makes a verbally aggressive outburst and/or a physically aggressive outburst.

(This phone call is coming from the principal's office. The principal and the teacher agree that the teacher will lead the phone conversation.)

"Hello! My name is…. I'm Jamie's teacher. Is now a good time for us to talk?"
Words of Respect

"I'm calling to share something that happened in class today. Jamie yelled out and threw a chair across the room."
Words of Accountability

"I talked with Jamie to get an understanding of his behavior. I asked him to help me understand why he yelled out and threw the chair. I asked him if he was frustrated or angry or didn't feel well."
Words of Understanding

"I have Jamie here in the principal's office with me. He's going to talk with you about what happened."
Words of Accountability

(Jamie tells his parents what happened and is truthful.)

"We have school policies to make sure our school is a safe place for everyone, and the school's policy is clear about the consequences for this type of behavior. (State your school's policy for this type of behavior.)"
Words of Accountability

"I want to get to the root of Jamie's behavior and for him to know that I'm not upset with him; however, his behavior was not acceptable—we can't accept this in our classroom."
Words of Understanding

"So, I wanted to reach out and make you aware of his behavior and work together to get to the bottom of what is going on with Jamie. Has Jamie shared anything with you about our class, or other students in our class, that could give us a better understanding of how he's feeling about school?"
Words of Understanding

"Before we finish our conversation, I wanted to share that I have enjoyed having Jamie in my class. He is . . . . . (share something personal, positive, and specific that you've experienced with Jamie)."
Words of Encouragement

"At the beginning of the school year at the parent Open House, you and I talked about the importance of maintaining a strong relationship and open communication between home and school."
Words of Relationship

"If you can think of anything we can do to make things better for Jamie, please let me know. My hope is for all of our students to feel safe, enjoy school, and learn every day."
Words of Hope

GTL Classroom Activities to Transform Student Behavior and Your Classroom Culture

GTL Classroom Activities for Student Outbursts

We see these activities as either "in the moment" or a time to circle up for classroom meetings to encourage student voice and student engagement in your classroom. We see the teacher as a facilitator and co-learner during these GTL activities and students as active participants in learning how to "see the classroom through the lens of the teacher" and how to manage their own behavior.

1. (Role-Play GTL Scenario for "This Is So Boring!") Select one student to role-play a teacher and two other students to role-play two students who are talking about how the class is so boring and one student yells out, "This Is So Boring!" Encourage the other students in the class to help the role-playing teacher with what to say and how to respond to the outburst.
2. (Hit the Pause Button for Class Discussion on "Why Do We Have to Learn This?") Share with the students that you are going to "Hit the Pause Button" on the lesson and take important time to discuss *why* we need to learn this information. Ask the whole class for their personal answers for *why* they think this lesson is important and how they might use it in the future: "Why do you think we need to learn this?" Conclude the discussion by adding your personal reasons for *why* this lesson is important.
3. (Revisiting the Classroom Rules and Behavior Expectations about "Profanity") Remind the students about "Our Classroom Rules and Behavior Expectations" that everyone helped create and agreed to follow. Spend time discussing the rules about profanity and why it is inappropriate and the consequences for the inappropriate outburst. Privately discuss the consequences of the profanity outburst with the student and follow school policy.

7

What Do Great Teachers Say When a Student Does Not Show Respect for Themselves or Others?

What do you say when your students do not show respect for themselves, their classmates and/or you? This chapter provides teacher-friendly charts with Great Teacher Language (GTL) Reminders to Self, GTL to Share with Students, GTL to Use When Talking and Communicating with Parents, and GTL Classroom Activities specifically related to the following:

Scenario 7.1: A student is calling other students names and/or making fun of other students.
Scenario 7.2: A student is making inappropriate gestures at other students and/or the teacher.
Scenario 7.3: A student is verbally disrespectful to the teacher.
Scenario 7.4: A student is interrupting another student and/or the teacher.
Scenario 7.5: A student is taking things that do not belong to him/her.
Scenario 7.6: A student is demonstrating a lack of self-respect.

DOI: 10.4324/9781003400141-8

> We know these are not the only disrespectful behaviors that happen in your classroom. These specific scenarios are a starting point for you to develop your Great Teacher Language (GTL) for your classroom. For some of our student behavior scenarios, we have included GTL examples for you to use when talking with parents. These GTL examples are templates for phone conversations, emails, or other types of messages to develop strong communication between teachers and parents and to promote understanding, relationships, trust, and collaboration.

Respect has a powerful ripple effect on those around us. When we give respect, we often get respect in return. When we respect students, they feel empowered, valued, and needed. When students feel respected, they are more likely to demonstrate respect for themselves and others. Disrespectful behaviors disrupt class and impede learning. Your Language of Practice (LoP) in the form of GTL can create a culture of mutual respect and offer these disrespectful students the accountability, encouragement, grace, guidance, high expectations, hope, love, relationships, respect, understanding, and unity necessary to successfully engage them in the learning.

Teachers and students often jointly create a rule for their classroom: Be respectful. But do students know what respect is? Do they know what good examples of respect look like and sound like in your classroom? If left undefined, respect is a concept that can be abstract for students. The meaning of "respect" is often left open for interpretation, and students develop their own understandings of what it means to them. It is important for teachers to offer a clear definition and concrete examples of true respect. (See GTL Classroom Activities at the end of this chapter.)

We believe students show true respect when they choose to demonstrate a proper regard for the dignity of their own character and the character of others. It reveals an intentional consideration and appreciation of others. It is so important for teachers to use Words of Respect, demonstrate respect toward their students, and highlight examples of student respect when they occur.

Students might not have a clear understanding of what respect is, but they certainly know what disrespect looks like and sounds like! They also know what disrespect feels like. How do you feel and respond when you are disrespected? If we react to disrespect with disrespect, it can cause a cycle of bigger problems. When students are being disrespectful, our language and actions can certainly make things better or worse.

Disrespectful behaviors are like encrypted messages indicating deeper problems. What if we decoded these messages from the student as: "It's not because I am a bad kid—I'm just struggling, and I need your help. If we could get to the reason for my disrespect and help me eliminate it, I could be a good kid." Why do students choose to be disrespectful to others? What are the underlying reasons? Some students show disrespect to others because they themselves are victims of disrespect. Their feelings of powerlessness and helplessness result in outward disrespect as they seek to overpower and control the teacher or other students. Other disrespectful behavior is an indication of students feeling angry, threatened, insecure, jealous, or seeking revenge.

Understanding why students choose disrespect can help us in guiding students to choose other behaviors. If we identify the underlying reason for disrespect, we can separate the student from their behavior and work to eliminate the reason for their disrespectful behavior. When we recognize the underlying reason for the outward show of disrespect, it says to students, "I am here to help you."

What about the students with a lack of self-respect? Are there outward signs that indicate how they feel on the inside? How can we help them? When students feel inadequate, unworthy, or afraid of failure, they may experience a lack of self-respect. This lack of self-respect results in a wide range of behaviors from subtle to extremely obvious. Some students attempt to become invisible, whereas others seek to be the center of attention. Their class participation may be limited or overbearing as they seek to overcompensate for their feelings of inadequacy. When students feel insecure or unworthy, they often choose reactions that show disrespect toward themselves. These self-disrespecting behaviors can negatively impact learning for the student.

Building and maintaining a culture of mutual respect are essential for student safety and success. This begins with teachers who model respect. When students see us being respectful, they begin to understand what respect really looks like, sounds like, and how they can show respect for themselves and others. When students and teachers demonstrate respect for one another, the classroom becomes a safe environment for learning and success.

We all want respect from others, and when we freely give it, we expect it in return. However, when we show others respect and get disrespect in return, it creates a discouraging situation and a stormy environment. Trust is lost and relationships are damaged. Fostering a culture of mutual respect in your classroom helps to eliminate these stormy situations. The ultimate goal is for students to demonstrate respect intentionally and to make a conscious decision to show consideration and appreciation for their classmates, their teachers, and others.

WHAT DO GREAT TEACHERS SAY WHEN...?

A Student is Calling Other Students Names And/Or Making Fun of Other Students. (Scenario 7.1)

GTL Reminders to Self:

Remember... Respectful actions are contagious.
Words of Hope

Remember... Students need to see and hear "concrete" examples of what respect looks like and sounds like.
Words of Guidance

Remember... Some students show disrespect to others and make fun of other students because they have been made fun of by someone else.
Words of Understanding

Remember... Some disrespectful behavior is an indication of students feeling angry, threatened, insecure, jealous, or seeking revenge.
Words of Understanding

GTL to Share with Students:

(Whole class) "When all of your friends are making fun of somebody, it can be tough to do the right thing.

I trust that you will make the right decision and show respect to everyone."
Words of Accountability

(Whispering to student) "How would you feel if someone said that to you? How do you feel when someone disrespects you?"
Words of Understanding

"Today, I want us to discuss the importance of respect. Why is it important to show respect for each other?"
Words of Understanding

"We are all unique! Even though we dress differently or speak differently—those differences are no reason to be disrespectful."
Words of Unity

"In our classroom, we want to establish a climate where no one feels embarrassed to say one thing or another. We will work together to respect each other's opinions and thoughts."
Words of Unity

"We all make mistakes. At some point, everybody in this class—including me—will do something that causes us to feel embarrassed. Let's promise not to make fun of others when this happens and make it worse for them."
Words of Grace

"When someone does something to hurt your feelings, it is important to talk with them about it. Once you have discussed it with them and they have apologized, let's all promise to forgive and forget."
Words of Grace

GTL to Use When Talking and Communicating with Parents:

Phone call to discuss a student's behavior in the classroom: A student is calling other students names and/or making

fun of other students, which distracts from the lesson and is causing the other students to be upset.

(Note: This GTL phone conversation provides a template you can modify and send to parents as a letter, email, text message, etc.).

"Hello! My name is…. I'm Jamie's teacher. He's not in trouble. Is now a good time for us to talk?"

Words of Respect

"I enjoy having Jamie in my class. He is… (share something personal, positive, and specific that you've experienced with Jamie)."

Words of Encouragement

"Since the first day of school, we have been talking about respectful behaviors in the classroom and the importance of showing respect to one another. I'm calling you to share something that happened today. Jamie was calling other students names and making fun of them in the classroom."

Words of Accountability

"I talked with Jamie to get an understanding about his behavior. I also asked Jamie if other students have been calling him names or making fun of him. He told me that no one was calling him names or making fun of him."

Words of Understanding

"I wanted to mention this to you and let you know about this issue. I encouraged Jamie to apologize to the other students. I am so proud of Jamie because he did apologize, and he and the other students were able to continue the activity together."

Words of Unity

"Please let me know if you have any questions at all. My hope is for all of our students to feel safe, enjoy school, and learn every day."

Words of Hope

WHAT DO GREAT TEACHERS SAY WHEN...?

A Student is Making Inappropriate Gestures At Other Students And/Or The Teacher. (Scenario 7.2)

GTL Reminders to Self:

Remember... When you take student disrespect personally, you can lose sight of a possible solution to solve a bigger problem.

Words of Understanding

Remember... When you model respect, it can change your students' way of thinking and acting.

Words of Guidance

Remember... If you don't hold students accountable in the moment, it can lead to a classroom environment where students become accustomed to constant meaningless reminders, fail to see their impact on others, and start to do what they want to do.

Words of Accountability

Remember... When students and teachers demonstrate respect for one another, the classroom becomes a safe environment for learning and success.

Words of Encouragement

GTL to Share with Students:

"I care about you, so I am going to hold you accountable for the choices you make."

Words of Love

(Whispering to the student) "Right now, you might not like me as your teacher, but I do deserve your respect, and I am going to respect you."

Words of Respect

(Whole class after a class game) "Whether you win or lose, we need to promise to be supportive of each other and congratulate the winners. Good character and sportsmanship show that we are able to win with character and lose with dignity."

Words of Encouragement

"As a class, let's discuss how to respect each other. What does it look like and sound like when we show respect for someone?"

Word of Understanding

"That was very unkind and disrespectful. How could you have handled that differently?"

Words of Accountability

"Even when you're disrespectful and you misbehave, I want to help you. I want you to be successful, so let's figure out a way for that to happen."

Words of Grace

GTL to Use When Talking and Communicating with Parents:

Phone call to discuss a student's behavior in the classroom: A student is making inappropriate gestures at other students and/or the teacher.

(Note: This GTL phone conversation provides a template you can modify and send to parents as a letter, email, text message, etc.).

"Hello! My name is…. I'm Jamie's teacher. Is now a good time for us to talk?"

Words of Respect

"I'm calling you to share something that happened today at school. Jamie made an inappropriate gesture toward me in class. (State the specific inappropriate behavior.)"

Words of Accountability

"I talked with Jamie to get an understanding about his behavior. I wanted him to know that I'm not upset

with him; however, his behavior was not acceptable—we can't accept this in our classroom."
Words of Understanding

"So, I wanted to reach out and make you aware of his behavior and work together to get to the bottom of what is going on with Jamie. Has Jamie shared anything with you about me, or about our class, that could give us a better understanding of how he's feeling about school?"
Words of Understanding

"We have school policies to make sure our school is a safe place for everyone, and the school's policy is clear about inappropriate gestures. (State your school's policy for this type of behavior.)"
Words of Accountability

"Before we finish our conversation, I wanted to share that I have enjoyed having Jamie in my class. He is… (share something personal, positive, and specific that you've experienced with Jamie)."
Words of Encouragement

"At the beginning of the school year at the parent Open House, we talked about the importance of maintaining a strong relationship and open communication between home and school."
Words of Relationship

"If you can think of anything we can do to make things better for Jamie, please let me know. My hope is for all of our students to feel safe, enjoy school, and learn every day."
Words of Hope

WHAT DO GREAT TEACHERS SAY WHEN...?

A Student is Verbally Disrespectful to the Teacher. (Scenario 7.3)

GTL Reminders to Self:

Remember... Don't allow disrespectful student behavior to become a personal conflict—you vs. student. Keep the focus on helping the student and not on defending yourself or maintaining power, saving face, and so on.

Words of Unity

Remember... It's rare for students to hear an authority figure say 'I'm sorry' or 'I made a mistake.' This honest and transparent action teaches them that an apology can restore a relationship and is the right thing to do.

Words of Relationship

Remember... When we are dealing with disrespectful behaviors, students need to see and hear a consistency in our actions and our language.

Words of Accountability

Remember... When students talk back and disrespect you, it is an important time for you to provide a respectful response that creates a safe and accountable environment and shows the student that you care about them.

Words of Love

GTL to Share with Students:

"We are not always going to agree, but when we have disagreements, we owe each other respect."

Words of Respect

"When I disagree with you, I'm going to do my best to model for you what it sounds like to respectfully disagree with someone."

Words of Guidance

"Everybody in our classroom is different, and we will not always agree with each other, but everyone deserves our respect and kindness."
Words of Unity

"I understand what you are saying, but I don't agree with it. Let's agree to disagree and keep the conversation going."
Word of Respect

(Whispering to a student) "I don't like it when you talk back to me and disrespect me, but I still care about you."
Words of Grace

"We really need to watch what we say. Words do matter."
Words of Respect

GTL to Use When Talking and Communicating with Parents:

Phone call to discuss a student's behavior in the classroom: A student is verbally disrespectful to you.

(Note: This GTL phone conversation provides a template you can modify and send to parents as a letter, email, text message, and so on. You will notice this GTL phone call conversation is very similar to the previous GTL phone call for: *A student is making inappropriate gestures at other students and/or the teacher*. We hope the GTL similarities will provide you with a GTL framework and a working template for future phone calls with parents to maintain a strong relationship and open communication between home and school.)

"Hello! My name is .... I'm Jamie's teacher. Is now a good time for us to talk?"
Words of Respect

"I'm calling you to share something that happened today at school. Jamie was verbally disrespectful to me in class. (State the specific inappropriate behavior.)"
Words of Accountability

"I talked with Jamie to get an understanding about his behavior. I wanted him to know that I'm not upset with him; however, his language was not acceptable—we can't accept this in our classroom."
Words of Understanding

"So, I wanted to reach out and make you aware of his behavior and work together to get to the bottom of what is going on with Jamie. Has Jamie shared anything with you about me, or about our class, that could give us a better understanding of how he's feeling about school?"
Words of Understanding

"We have school policies to make sure our school is a safe place for everyone, and the school's policy is clear about a student's verbal disrespect to teachers. (State your school's policy for this type of behavior.)"
Words of Accountability

"Before we finish our conversation, I wanted to share that I have enjoyed having Jamie in my class. He is… (share something personal, positive, and specific that you've experienced with Jamie)."
Words of Encouragement

"At the beginning of the school year at the parent Open House, we talked about the importance of maintaining a strong relationship and open communication between home and school."
Words of Relationship

"If you can think of anything we can do to make things better for Jamie, please let me know. My hope is for all of our students to feel safe, enjoy school, and learn every day."
Words of Hope

WHAT DO GREAT TEACHERS SAY WHEN...?

A Student is Interrupting Another Student And/Or the Teacher. (Scenario 7.4)

GTL Reminders to Self:

Remember... You cannot expect respect without being willing to give it.

Words of Respect

Remember... By talking with students respectfully, you give them the sense of 'Maybe this teacher cares.'

Words of Love

Remember... Love and respect for students in spite of what they do is grace in action.

Words of Grace

GTL to Share with Students:

(Share with the whole class) "I am responsible for making sure all of you have the chance to learn and the chance to complete your assignments without disruptions. As your teacher, I am accountable for what goes on in this classroom, and showing respect for one another is expected every day."

Words of High Expectations

"I can't wait to hear what all of you think about our topic today. Let's remember to listen to everyone and give them our full attention."

Words of Unity

"I appreciate how you waited to speak and gave the other students your attention while they were speaking. That was an act of respect for others."

Words of Encouragement

"It is so important to respect others by listening when they are speaking in class."

Words of Respect

"If someone makes a mistake in our classroom, it is important to think about how you react to that mistake. In our classroom, we will treat others the way we want to be treated."

Words of Understanding

"Please watch yourself and do not interrupt or distract others while they're working on assignments."

Words of Guidance

WHAT DO GREAT TEACHERS SAY WHEN...?

A Student Is Taking Things That Do Not Belong to Him/Her. (Scenario 7.5)

GTL Reminders to Self:

Remember... Students have lots of different reasons for taking things that do not belong to them. They take food because they are hungry, they take a pencil because they don't have one, they take things because they want what they don't have, and sometimes they take things for a deeper reason.

Words of Understanding

Remember... Your students are watching how you model respect for other teachers, parents, students, and the principal. What you 'say and do' can be a great model of the respect that you expect to see from them. Words of Respect

Remember... Students will make some poor choices at times and need to be redirected.

Words of Grace

Remember... Establishing mutual respect within your classroom will help your students to respect each other's belongings.

Words of Unity

Remember... Encourage students to share with you when they need something, such as food, pencils, or paper.

Words of Love

GTL to Share with Students:

"It's so important to respect other students' belongings. We need to remember that what your other classmates have is not yours, and if you would like to see it or use it, you will need to ask their permission."

Words of Respect

"If you need something you don't have, before you take something that does not belong to you, please remember to ask me if I can help you."

Words of Love

"All it takes is for one person to understand the importance of respecting other people's belongings to start a culture of mutual respect in our classroom. I'm going to encourage each of you to be that first person."

Words of Encouragement

"In our classroom, we want to be able to trust one another. I'm going to be honest with you, and I hope you will all be honest with me. If you take something that doesn't belong to you, it's important to take personal responsibility and return it. That's an act of integrity and will help restore our trust with one another."

Words of Relationship

"I really appreciate your honesty. When you are honest with me, it shows me that you respect yourself enough to tell the truth."

Words of Encouragement

GTL to Use When Talking and Communicating with Parents:

Phone call to discuss a student's behavior in the classroom: A student is taking things that do not belong to him/her.

(Note: This GTL phone conversation provides a template you can modify and send to parents as a letter, email, text message, etc.).

"Hello! My name is …. I'm Jamie's teacher. Is now a good time for us to talk?"
Words of Respect

"I'm calling you to share something that happened today at school. A student came to me and said that Jamie took something from him that did not belong to Jamie."
Words of Accountability

"I talked with Jamie to find out what exactly was going on and to get his side of the story."
Words of Understanding

"Jamie admitted that he took the item from the other student. I was proud of Jamie's honesty."
Words of Encouragement

"We are teaching students that it's so important to respect other students' belongings. They need to remember that what their other classmates have is not theirs, and if they would like to see it or use it, they need to ask for permission. Our goal is to promote mutual respect in our classroom."
Words of Guidance

"We have school policies to make sure our school is a safe place for everyone, and the school's policy is clear about taking things that belong to other students. (State your school's policy for this type of behavior.)"
Words of Accountability

"I wanted you to know that I encourage students to let me know when they need something they might have forgotten at home that day, like pencils, paper, a snack, and other things they might need."

Words of Love

"Please let me know if you have any questions at all. My hope is for all of our students to feel safe, enjoy school, and learn every day."

Words of Hope

WHAT DO GREAT TEACHERS SAY WHEN...?

A Student is Demonstrating a Lack of Self-Respect. (Scenario 7.6)

GTL Reminders to Self:

Remember... Talking individually with students gives us greater insight into their life, their thoughts, and their needs.

Words of Relationship

Remember... Students need a teacher who wants the best for them, who is looking out for them, and who is guiding them in love all along the way.

Words of Love

Remember... When students feel inadequate, unworthy, or afraid of failure, they may experience a lack of self-respect. This lack of self-respect results in a wide range of behaviors from subtle to extremely obvious.

Words of Understanding

Remember... When students have low self-respect, look for their positive behaviors to celebrate.

Words of High Expectations

GTL to Share with Students:

(Use this GTL when you want to help a student shift from a lack of self-respect mindset to a self-respect mindset. You can personalize it for the specific student.) "I've noticed you're really good at art. I could use your help with this new bulletin board. Could you help me think about how to design it?"

Words of Understanding

"I believe in you. Even though you might not think you can do this, I believe you can."

Words of Love

(When students have low self-respect, look for positive behaviors to celebrate. You can personalize this GTL for the specific student.) "I really appreciate and respect how you have helped make our new student feel welcomed this week."

Words of Encouragement

(Whispering to student) "Don't be so hard on yourself. I still have faith in your abilities, and I believe that you can do better."

Words of Grace

"If you don't respect yourself, then it's almost impossible for you to respect others."

Words of Respect

GTL to Use When Talking and Communicating with Parents:

Phone call to discuss a student's behavior in the classroom: A student is demonstrating a lack of self-respect—a student is being too hard on himself.

(Note: This GTL phone conversation provides a template you can modify and send to parents as a letter, email, text message, etc.).

"Hello! My name is .... I'm Jamie's teacher. He's not in trouble. Is now a good time for us to talk?"

Words of Respect

"I enjoy having Jamie in my class. He is… (share something personal, positive, and specific that you've experienced with Jamie)."
Words of Encouragement

"I'm calling you to share something that I noticed today at school. Jamie was really hard on himself when we were working on a class activity. He said multiple times that 'I can't do this, I'm too stupid'."
Words of Accountability

"I talked with Jamie to get an understanding about his behavior. I wanted him to know that I think he is very capable of doing the work, and I'm here to help him when it gets challenging."
Words of Understanding

"In our classroom, our goal is to promote mutual respect. We talk about the importance of self-respect and respecting others, and I wanted to reach out and make you aware of his behavior and work together to get to the bottom of what is going on with Jamie."
Words of Understanding

"At the beginning of the school year at the parent Open House, we talked about the importance of maintaining a strong relationship and open communication between home and school."
Words of Relationship

"If you can think of anything we can do to make things better for Jamie, please let me know. My hope is for all of our students to feel safe, enjoy school, and learn every day."
Words of Hope

GTL Classroom Activities to Transform Student Behavior and Your Classroom Culture

GTL Classroom Activities for Students Who Do Not Show Respect for Themselves and Others

We see these activities as either "in the moment" or a time to circle up for classroom meetings to encourage student voice and student engagement in your classroom. We see the teacher as a facilitator and co-learner during these GTL activities and students as active participants in learning how to "see the classroom through the lens of the teacher" and how to manage their own behavior.

1. (Role-Play GTL Scenario for students who are demonstrating a lack of self-respect and being hard on themselves.) Select one student to role-play a teacher and one student to role-play a student who is demonstrating a lack of self-respect and being hard on himself/herself. Allow time for the student to role-play his/her lack of self-respect by saying things like "I can't do this, I'm too stupid." Allow time for the role-playing teacher to share encouraging and respectful words with the student. After the role-play, ask the self-disrespecting student if what the role-playing teacher said was helpful. Encourage the other students in the class to help the role-playing teacher with what to say and how to respectfully respond to the student to help them shift from a lack of self-respect to self-respect. Conclude the role-playing activity with a discussion of how you, as the teacher, can respectfully help students shift from a lack of self-respect to self-respect.
2. (Hit the Pause Button for Discussion on Promoting Mutual Respect in the Classroom when you see multiple students *being respectful*.) Share with the students that you are going to "Hit the Pause Button" on the lesson and take important time to share with the students the respectful behavior you saw and the respectful language you heard from students today and put their respectful behaviors/

language on the Creating Mutual Respect Chart. Ask students to think about examples of respectful behavior and respectful language that they have heard this week. Allow time for each student to share one of their examples and put them on the Creating Mutual Respect Chart. Conclude the discussion by sharing how you and the students will continue to add respectful behavior and language to the chart.

3. (Revisiting the Classroom Rules and Behavior Expectations about "Respecting Other Students' Belongings.") Remind the students about "Our Classroom Rules and Behavior Expectations" that everyone helped create and agreed to follow. Spend some time discussing the importance of respecting other students' belongings. Remind students that if they would like to see or use something that does not belong to them, they need to ask for permission from the other student. Share with students the importance of honesty and how we want to be able to trust one another. Emphasize with students that if they take something that doesn't belong to them, it's important to take personal responsibility and return the item. That's an act of integrity and will help restore trust with one another. Conclude the discussion by reassuring the students that if they need something they don't have, then they can ask you, as the teacher, to help them.

8

What Do Great Teachers Say When a Student Refuses to Cooperate or Challenges Them?

What do you say when a student refuses to cooperate or challenges you (e.g., questions your decisions, questions your authority, refuses to do work, confronts you in front of the class, or demonstrates blatant disrespect). This chapter provides teacher-friendly charts with Great Teacher Language (GTL) Reminders to Self, GTL to Share with Students, GTL to Use When Talking and Communicating with Parents, and GTL Classroom Activities specifically related to the following:

Scenario 8.1: A student consistently asks questions that challenge you and/or the lesson you are teaching.

Scenario 8.2: A student says, "I don't agree with you" or "I don't believe you" or "You are wrong!"

Scenario 8.3: A student refuses to cooperate with you and says, "You're not my mom. You can't tell me what to do! You can't make me do this work!"

Scenario 8.4: A student is outwardly angry and blatantly disrespectful toward you.

> We know these are not the only uncooperative or challenging behaviors that happen in your classroom. These specific scenarios are a starting point for you to develop your Great Teacher Language (GTL) for your classroom. For some of our student behavior scenarios, we have included GTL examples for you to use when talking with parents. These GTL examples are templates for phone conversations, emails, or other types of messages to develop strong communication between teachers and parents and to promote understanding, relationships, trust, and collaboration.

When students refuse to cooperate and challenge us in the classroom, it is important to get to the root of the problem and ask ourselves:

- Is this student frustrated with me, or is the student trying to make sense of the material?
- Is this student's disagreeable behavior toward me their way of sharing their own opinion?
- Is this student feeling threatened in some way and setting up a power struggle with me?
- Is this the student's way of telling me they are angry about something?

Our GTL goal is to help uncooperative and challenging students experience a learning environment that supports and encourages (1) critical thinking, (2) mutual respect where all students feel free to share their own opinions respectfully, (3) win-win relational outcomes between the teacher and students, and (4) personal strategies for students to defuse their anger and defiance before they impact their learning. Your Language of Practice (LoP) in the form of GTL can offer these uncooperative or challenging students the accountability, encouragement, grace, guidance, high expectations, hope, love, relationships, respect, understanding, and unity they need in the moment and beyond.

Scenario 8.1: A student consistently asks questions that challenge you and/or the lesson you are teaching.

When students are asking so many questions about the lesson and their questioning seems rude or arrogant, we can feel challenged and may get defensive. When their critical thinking and questioning are disrespectful, it is important to hold these students accountable for their disrespectful behaviors. As we work with these critical thinkers, we need to approach them carefully to ensure their respect for us and our respect for their curiosity. When they question why they need to learn the material, we need to be ready to tell them why. When they ask questions over and over, we need to help them make sense of what they are learning. We also need to answer them honestly if we do not know the answer to their questions: "I don't know, but let's find out together." As we work toward our GTL goal to encourage critical thinking and critical thinkers, the students need to see that we are learners, too. These questions can be an opportunity for us to say, "That's a great question. I've never thought about it that way."

Scenario 8.2: A student says, "I don't agree with you" or "I don't believe you" or "You are wrong!"

A GTL goal for your classroom is to promote open and honest classroom discussions, where students can develop and share their own opinions. As students feel the freedom to share their opinions, some students might feel the freedom to disrespectfully disagree with you in front of the class. When students share their opinions disrespectfully or are being disrespectfully disagreeable with you, it is important to hold them accountable for their disrespect, redirect them back to the lesson, and remind them of the class expectation of showing mutual respect. Mutual respect is shown when we value everyone as a person, show respect for everyone's opinion, and share our own opinion respectfully. As we work with disrespectfully opinionated and disagreeable students, it is important to address their disrespectful opinions and disagreeable attitudes, while we value their input and be ready to help them see other points of view. These disagreements can be an opportunity for us to say, "That's an interesting way to think about it. I've never thought about it that way. I don't agree with you, but in order for us to move ahead in our lesson, we need to agree to disagree for now. I respect you and want to hear more about your opinion. Let's talk more after class."

Scenario 8.3: A student refuses to cooperate with you and says, "You're not my mom. You can't tell me what to do! You can't make me do this work!"

Have you ever heard these words? What did you say? What did you want to say? It is usually our inclination to fight power with power, especially when we are the authority in the classroom. However, we believe it is important to always avoid a power struggle with a student. Giving back to students what they give you and trying to overpower them constitute a lose-lose situation and can derail learning in the classroom.

Coercion might seem to work in the short term. However, for long-term change—real change and real relationships—we propose that you adopt a more persuasive stance that says to students, "You are right. I can't make you do it. I can't make you do anything. It's not my job to make you do an assignment. It's my job to teach you and help you in any way I can. The choice is up to you." It is important for students to understand that the choice to cooperate is up to them and that they will be held accountable for their choices. If they do not complete an assignment or refuse to cooperate, there are consequences. If they do complete the assignment or choose to cooperate, there are different consequences. The choice is up to them. It is our responsibility to help them work through these consequences—good or bad—and learn from them. Our GTL goal is to help students become self-managed where they are empowered to make better choices for themselves and experience better consequences too.

This persuasive stance places the focus back on the students' freedom to choose their own behaviors and holds students accountable for their choices. So, if power struggles with students are a "lose-lose" proposition, then how do we get to a "win-win"? How do we prevent a "lose-lose" situation when students challenge us? If we use coercion to deal with the issue, then students can feel threatened, backed into a corner, ready for competition, and *not* ready for learning. They feel that decisions are being made for them, and they don't have a choice in the matter—they lose and we lose. If we ignore challenging and uncooperative students, then they continue with their poor choices without proper guidance—another lose-lose.

What does a "win-win" solution look like and sound like when a student is challenging and uncooperative? It is important to show and tell students that our goal is not to win the power struggle against them. Our GTL goal is to show them that we are on the same team—and our ultimate goal is their success! We experience success when our students find success. We believe a "win-win" solution occurs when we demonstrate to students that our intention is not "to work and fight against them" but rather to "work and fight for them." A "win-win" solution becomes more likely when students know we are on their side, we understand and validate their feelings, and we will work with them to find a solution.

Scenario 8.4: A student is outwardly angry and blatantly disrespectful toward you.

People get angry. It's unrealistic to think that everyone is going to be happy every day in our classroom. We can't stop students from being angry and disrespectful, but we can help students learn how to work through their anger and defiance to develop self-management. Without self-management, students act out their anger and defiance in the classroom and negatively impact the learning environment. It is important for teachers to get to know their students and build trusting relationships that will lead to personal conversations about the causes of their anger and defiance. When a student shares their anger and defiance triggers with the teacher, this honest realization is the first step toward self-management. Then the teacher and student together can develop personal self-management strategies to stop the anger and defiance before they start. Self-management also prevents anger and defiance from escalating into more verbally and physically aggressive student behaviors.

When students come to school with anger and defiance already overwhelming them, or they become angry at school, we can see it in their faces and hear it in the tone of their voices. Often their anger and defiance lead to behaviors and emotions that push teachers further away and perpetuate feelings of isolation and rebellion. These students really need for us to see them fully—and recognize and address both their inappropriate behaviors and their need for our care and support. It is important for our words and actions to convey to students that we are on the lookout for these warning signs—ready to offer grace, guidance, accountability, and hope—and ready to say to them, "I am aware, and I care."

WHAT DO GREAT TEACHERS SAY WHEN…?

A Student Consistently Asks Questions That Challenge You And/Or the Lesson You Are Teaching. (Scenario 8.1)

GTL Reminders to Self:

Remember… Grace is a powerful way to show patience and love for students who seem to be challenging you.
Words of Grace

Remember… Instead of admonishing students for asking questions that challenge you or the lesson you are teaching, offer them assistance and clearer guidance about how to respectfully ask their questions.
Words of Guidance

Remember… When students are asking you challenging questions, it doesn't always mean they are challenging your authority.
Words of Understanding

Remember… It's important to promote critical thinking in your classroom. When you are teaching and students are really learning, some students may ask challenging questions that derail your lesson plan. As we work with these critical thinkers, we need to approach them carefully to ensure their respect for us and our respect for their curiosity.
Words of Respect

Remember… Take time to call parents and let them know when their child is excited about learning and curious about the topic you're teaching. This positive phone call is an excellent way to maintain a strong relationship and open communication between home and school.
Words of Unity

GTL to Share with Students:

"You're really thinking about this topic in such a great way. It's good because you are challenging me and your classmates to consider other possibilities."

Words of Encouragement

(Talking individually with a student) "You've got some great questions, but you need to work on how to ask them. It's hard to listen to your questions and comments when they are disrespectful. Let's talk about how you can ask the same questions in a different way."

Words of Guidance

"That's a great question—and, honestly, I don't know the answer. Let's work together and try to find the answer."

Words of Unity

"That is one way to think about it. Does anyone else have a different idea."

Words of Respect

"I really love your curiosity about this topic. You've made me want to learn more about it, too."

Words of Love

GTL to Use When Talking and Communicating with Parents:

Positive phone call to celebrate a student's behavior in your classroom: A student is demonstrating great curiosity and excitement about the lesson and asking excellent questions that motivate everyone's learning.

(Note: This GTL phone conversation provides a template you can modify and send to parents as a letter, email, text message, etc.).

"Hello! My name is…. I'm Jamie's teacher. He's not in trouble. Is now a good time for us to talk?"

Words of Respect

"I'm calling you to share something that I noticed today at school. Jamie has been so excited about what we are learning in science this week. He has been asking questions, sharing information he has learned on his own, and motivating his classmates to learn more, too."
Words of Encouragement

"Jamie has such a natural curiosity about science, and he is always so attentive in science class. He is such a great role model for the other students in our classroom. I am so proud of him and his desire to learn."
Words of Relationship

"I can see Jamie having a job in science one day."
Words of Hope

"At the beginning of the school year at the parent Open House, we talked about the importance of maintaining a strong relationship and open communication between home and school. That's why I called today to share the great news about Jamie."
Words of Relationship

"If you can think of anything we can do to make things better for Jamie, please let me know. My hope is for all our students to feel safe, enjoy school, and learn as much as they can every day."
Words of Hope

WHAT DO GREAT TEACHERS SAY WHEN...?

A Student Says, "I Don't Agree With You" Or "I Don't Believe You" Or "You Are Wrong!" (Scenario 8.2)

GTL Reminders to Self:

Remember... Sometimes, students think they can look cool or get an ego boost by challenging authority in front of their peers. Be careful not to get tangled in a war of words. Stay calm, remain professional, and do not allow your emotional buttons to get pushed.

Words of Guidance

Remember... Asking a student to consider a different point of view demonstrates respect, and telling a student their point of view is wrong demonstrates disrespect.

Words of Respect

Remember... As we work with disrespectfully opinionated and disagreeable students, it is important to hold them accountable for their disrespectful opinions and disagreeable attitudes, while we value their input and be ready to help them see other points of view.

Words of Grace

Remember... When students share their opinions disrespectfully or are being disrespectfully disagreeable with you, it is important to hold them accountable for their disrespect, redirect them back to the lesson, and remind them of the class expectation of showing mutual respect.

Words of Accountability

Remember... Don't be afraid to share with your students what matters most to you and about who you are (your family, your hobbies, your interests). Take time to get to know who your students are. Find out what motivates them and what they care about and enjoy. Once they get to know you better and connect with you, they might stop their disrespectful behavior toward you.

Words of Love

Remember... Involving parents in your classroom is an excellent way to impact the behavior of your students. When students see their parents involved at school, trusting you and supporting you, their own behavior toward you can improve.

Words of Unity

GTL to Share with Students:

(Whispering to a student) "That was not the best way to share your disagreement, but that's an interesting perspective. I've never thought about it that way. Let's talk about how you could have shared your disagreement more respectfully."

Words of Accountability

(Whispering to a student) "I understand that you're entitled to your own opinion, and I want you to be able to share it. However, the way you just expressed it to the class was inappropriate. There are so many ways to tell others how you are thinking and feeling without being disrespectful."

Words of Respect

"I think we have a misunderstanding. Let's discuss it."

Words of Understanding

"Hold on. Say that again. I really want to hear what you were saying—I never thought of it that way."

Words of Relationship

"To maintain classroom unity, it's really important that we talk through our disagreements with respect and understanding."

Words of Grace

WHAT DO GREAT TEACHERS SAY WHEN…?

A Student Refuses to Cooperate with You and Says, "You're Not My Mom. You Can't Tell Me What to Do! You Can't Make Me Do This Work!" (Scenario 8.3)

GTL Reminders to Self:

Remember… When students refuse to do their work in front of their peers, be careful not to respond with coercion. Stay calm, remain professional, and use persuasion to offer them a different way of thinking about the importance of the assigned work and why they need to do it.

Words of Guidance

Remember... Coercion might seem to work in the short term; however, for long-term and real change, consider persuasion instead.

Words of Hope

Remember... When students refuse to cooperate with you and refuse to do their work, maintain accountability for the student by responding with persuasion rather than coercion. Persuasion will make a personal connection that encourages personal responsibility instead of coercion which uses short repetitive reminders that students often ignore.

Words of Accountability

Remember... When students experience your consistent accountability and respectful guidance after refusing to do the work, it can encourage and motivate them to complete their work.

Words of Encouragement

Remember... When students complete their work successfully after refusing to do the work, it can encourage and motivate them to do even better work and demonstrate better behavior.

Words of Encouragement

Remember... When students feel coerced, they may start to tune out or give up.

Words of Relationship

Remember... For optimum learning to occur, think win-win so the teacher wins and the student wins. A win-win solution becomes more likely when students know we are on their side, we understand and validate their feelings, and we will work with them to find a solution.

Words of Relationship

Remember... If a student refuses to cooperate with you, don't allow it to become teacher versus student. Keep redirecting everyone back to the lesson and learning.

Words of High Expectations

Remember... When we use our power and authority to coerce students into doing something, it might provide a short-term quick fix, but it doesn't empower students to manage themselves for a lifetime.

Words of Respect

Remember... Antagonistic words are destructive; they build walls and cause people to act out in ways that can negatively impact learning and relationships. Constructive Words of Grace build relationships and cause people to act in ways that are more positive and uplifting.

Words of Grace

GTL to Share with Students:

"You're right. I can't make you do your work. It is your choice whether you do your work. My job is not to make you do your work. My job is to teach you how to do it and then help you along the way. Your job is to learn as much as you can and try your hardest to complete your work. Please let me know if you need my help."

Words of Accountability

"You're right. I can't make you do your work. However, remember this assignment is due on Wednesday. So let me know what your plan is for completing it and if you need my help."

Words of Accountability

(A student says, "You're not my mom. You can't tell me what to do!") "You're right. I am not your mom. But when you are in my classroom, I am responsible for you, and I care about you. My job is to work with your mom (and your family) to support you and help you learn as much as you can."

              Words of Love

"I agree. I can't make you do anything. I can respectfully offer you the choices to choose from—and hopefully you'll make the right choice!"

              Words of Respect

(A student who refuses to get started on a project) "This project might feel like too much work for you right now, but you'll be so happy and proud of yourself when it's done—and that you've done your best. Let me know if I can help."

              Words of Grace

(A student continuously says, "I am not going to do this work.") "Can you help me understand what it is about this work that keeps you from doing it? Is it too hard? Too easy? Are you not interested in it? Let's take some time now to work out a plan for helping you to do your work in our classroom."

             Words of Understanding

(Talking individually with a student) "I asked you to step outside the classroom because I didn't want to single you out in class. Your behavior just now was disrespectful to me, and it's not how we agreed to treat each other at the beginning of the year. Let's think through some reasons for why you said that."

              Words of Respect

(Whispering to a student) "Did I do or say something that might have made you say that?"

             Words of Understanding

"I noticed you've stopped doing your work today. When I was in elementary school, I remember I really struggled with (share a specific struggle you had), and I wanted to give up. I'm so glad that I didn't. I know you can do this—so don't give up!"

Words of Encouragement

GTL to Use When Talking and Communicating with Parents:

Proactive phone call to understand why a student is refusing to cooperate with you in the classroom.

(A student refuses to cooperate with you and says, "You're not my mom. You can't tell me what to do! You can't make me do this work!")

(Note: This GTL phone conversation provides a template you can modify and send to parents as a letter, email, text message, etc.).

"Hello! My name is …. I'm Jamie's teacher. He's not in trouble. Is now a good time for us to talk?"

Words of Respect

"I enjoy having Jamie in my class. He is… (share something personal, positive, and specific that you've experienced with Jamie)."

Words of Encouragement

"Since the first day of school, we have been talking about respectful behaviors in the classroom and the importance of showing respect to one another. We've also talked about the importance of keeping a positive teacher–student relationship. I'm calling you to share something that happened today. Jamie was refusing to do his work and was disrespectful to me about it."

Words of Accountability

"I talked with Jamie to get an understanding about his behavior. I asked Jamie to help me understand what it is about the work that keeps him from doing it: Was it too hard? Too easy? Was he not interested in it? I also asked him if there's anything I've said or done that would make him act this way."

Words of Understanding

"He didn't seem to want to talk with me about it, so I wanted to reach out to you to get a better understanding of how he's feeling about school and his work. Is there anything you can share or that you've heard him say that would help me know how to encourage Jamie with his schoolwork?"

Words of Unity

"At the beginning of the school year at the parent Open House, we talked about the importance of maintaining a strong relationship and open communication between home and school. That's why I called today to share this update about Jamie."

Words of Relationship

"If you can think of anything we can do to make things better for Jamie, please let me know. My hope is that all of our students will feel safe, enjoy school, and learn as much as they can every day."

Words of Hope

WHAT DO GREAT TEACHERS SAY WHEN...?

A Student is Outwardly Angry and Blatantly Disrespectful Toward You. (Scenario 8.4)

GTL Reminders to Self:

Remember... When addressing a blatantly disrespectful student, it is best to use quieter, respectful accountability statements (e.g., "Your behavior right now is not respectful, and we need to talk about what's going on.") rather than louder, disrespectful accountability statements.

Words of Accountability

Remember... If you hold a grudge toward a student who is blatantly disrespectful toward you, it can impact your ability to be objective in dealing with that student.

Words of Grace

Remember... Sometimes, defiance can be a sign of a student's difficulty with reading, a challenge with understanding a concept, or the lesson is boring to them.

Words of Understanding

Remember... Sometimes, when students feel powerless in other relationships, they displace their feelings of frustration and defiance with their other relationships and take it out on a teacher.

Words of Understanding

Remember... A sudden change in behavior or a pattern of aggression can indicate a student's need for your help and attention.

Words of Relationship

Remember... Our goal is to help students learn how to work through their anger and defiance to develop self-management.

Words of Hope

GTL to Share with Students:

"Jamie, that behavior is unacceptable, and it's not how we agreed to treat each other when we set up our classroom behavior expectations for how to respect one another."

Words of Accountability

(Student refuses to leave the classroom to discuss misbehavior) "I really believe this is a situation that we can work out without getting the principal involved. It's up to you. If we can't discuss this privately and respectfully in the hallway, then you don't leave me a choice. We'll have to go talk with the principal to find a solution."

Words of Respect

(Student returns from an out-of-school suspension for a disrespectful act toward you.) "We missed you—I am glad you are back."

Words of Grace

"It seems like you are having a hard time today. Help me understand what's going on."

Words of Understanding

(Shared with the whole class) "Whenever any of you start to get angry, I want you to know that I am here to help. So, if I ask you 'What's going on?', it's because I want to understand what is making you angry, so we can address it and you can keep learning in my class."

Words of High Expectations

(Quiter response to an angry and disrespectful student) "It seems like you might be struggling today? How can I help you work through what's troubling you today?"

Words of Hope

(Individual conversation with angry student) "I can see something has you really upset. We can discuss it together, or you can go to the guidance counselor to talk it out. I don't want to see your anger get you into trouble."

Words of Guidance

(Shared with the whole class) "When anger happens in our classroom, I don't want to respond to anyone's anger with my own anger. My goal is to stay calm and focus on how to help you work through your anger."

Words of Love

(Individual conversation with student) "If you are feeling angry when you get to school, you need to come and tell me. We can decide together how to solve your problem."
Words of Relationship

"I know you are angry, and I understand why you would feel that way. However, you and I need to talk about a way to help you control that anger."
Words of Guidance

(Whispering to a student) "It looks like you need to cool down. Why don't you and I go out in the hallway and try to talk calmly?"
Words of Love

GTL to Use When Talking and Communicating with Parents:

Phone call to discuss a student's behavior in the classroom: A student is angry and blatantly disrespectful toward you.

(Note: This GTL phone conversation provides a template you can modify and send to parents as a letter, email, text message, etc.).

"Hello! My name is …. I'm Jamie's teacher. Is now a good time for us to talk?"
Words of Respect

"I'm calling to share something that happened today at school. Jamie was angry and disrespectful toward me in class. (State the specific inappropriate behavior.)"
Words of Accountability

"I talked with Jamie to get an understanding about his behavior. I asked Jamie to help me understand why he was so angry. I asked him if he was angry with me or with another student or if he was angry about the work. I also asked him if there's anything I've said or done that would make him act this way."
Words of Understanding

"I want to get to the root of Jamie's anger and for him to know that I'm not upset with him; however, his behavior was not acceptable—we can't accept this in our classroom."
Words of Understanding

"So, I wanted to reach out and make you aware of his behavior and work together to get to the bottom of what is going on with Jamie. Has Jamie shared anything with you about me, or about our class, that could give us a better understanding of how he's feeling about school?"
Words of Understanding

"We have school policies to make sure our school is a safe place for everyone, and the school's policy is clear about a student's blatant disrespect to a teacher. (State your school's policy for this type of behavior.)"
Words of Accountability

"Before we finish our conversation, I wanted to share that I have enjoyed having Jamie in my class. He is… (share something personal, positive, and specific that you've experienced with Jamie)."
Words of Encouragement

"At the beginning of the school year at the parent Open House, we talked about the importance of maintaining a strong relationship and open communication between home and school."
Words of Relationship

"If you can think of anything we can do to make things better for Jamie, please let me know. My hope is for all of our students to feel safe, enjoy school, and learn every day."
Words of Hope

GTL Classroom Activities to Transform Student Behavior and Your Classroom Culture

GTL Classroom Activities for Students who are Uncooperative or Challenge You

We see these activities as either "in the moment" or a time to circle up for classroom meetings to encourage student voice and student engagement in your classroom. We see the teacher as a facilitator and co-learner during these GTL activities and students as active participants in learning how to "see the classroom through the lens of the teacher" and how to manage their own behavior.

1. What does a Win-Win Teacher–Student Relationship Look Like and Sound Like? (Role-Play GTL Scenario for students who are disrespectfully disagreeing with the teacher and determine a Win-Win Teacher–Student outcome.) Select one student to role-play a teacher and one student to role-play a student who disrespectfully disagrees with the teacher and says, "That's not right, I don't agree with you." Allow time for the role-playing teacher to respond to the disrespectful student. After the role-play, ask the students who "won" the role-play. Did the teacher win? Why or why not? Did the student win? Why or why not? What does it sound like and look like for the teacher *and* the student to win? Encourage the other students in the class to help the role-playing teacher with what to say and how to respectfully respond to the disrespectful student for a win-win solution. The teacher will provide a win-win solution if the students do not provide win-win examples. Conclude the role-playing activity with a discussion of how you, as the teacher, have a goal for always having win-win outcomes for every situation in the classroom. You could also use other student misbehavior examples for this scenario. (For example, a student is blatantly disrespectful toward you or a student refuses to do their work.)

2. (Hit the Pause Button for Discussion on Encouraging Students' Self-Management of Anger when you see students displaying signs of anger in the classroom and toward you.) Share with the students that you are going to "Hit the Pause Button" on the lesson and take important time to discuss self-management strategies for dealing with anger to ensure the best learning and caring environment possible. Ask students to think of examples of self-management strategies they have used to prevent and deal with their own anger. Allow time for each student to share one of their examples and put them on the "Self-management strategies to prevent and deal with anger" chart. Conclude the discussion by sharing how your goal is to help them develop personal self-management strategies that will prevent anger and defiance before they start. Encourage students to always feel free to share with you their frustrations and needs in a one-on-one conversation, with a personal note to you, or in their personal reflection journals that you will read.
3. (Revisiting the Classroom Rules and Behavior Expectations for "What You Can Expect from Me as Your Teacher and What I Can Expect from You as a Student".) Remind the students about the "What You Can Expect from Me as Your Teacher and What I Can Expect from You as a Student" list that everyone helped create and agreed to follow and that's posted on the classroom wall. Spend time reviewing the teacher expectation list. The expectations for the teacher list could include the following:

As your teacher,
- I will respect and care for you.
- I will be prepared to teach you every day.
- I will not embarrass you in front of the class.
- I will be here to help you when you need me.
- I will listen to you and encourage you.
- I am going to challenge you to work hard and make good choices.

- I am going to teach you new things this year, and I'll help you learn them.
- I am going to always be looking for win-win solutions for every situation.
- I am going to connect with your parents this year.

    Spend time reviewing the student expectations list. The expectations for the student list could include the following:

As a student,
- I will respect the teacher and other students.
- I will be prepared and try hard to learn something new every day.
- I will work to get along with everyone.
- I will not embarrass my classmates or my teacher.
- I will make good choices.
- I will focus on learning.
- I will pay attention during lessons.
- I will avoid distractions.
- If I need help, I'll ask for help.
- I will work for win-win solutions with the teacher and other students.

Talk about the lists you have created and discuss if anything needs to be added. Remind students how following these high expectations for each other will maximize learning for everybody.

9

What Do Great Teachers Say When a Student Conflict Occurs?

What do you say when you observe a conflict between two students in your classroom (e.g., verbal argument, pushing and shoving, bullying, or a physical fight)? This chapter provides teacher-friendly charts with Great Teacher Language (GTL) Reminders to Self, GTL to Share with Students, GTL to Use When Talking and Communicating with Parents, and GTL Classroom Activities specifically related to the following:

Scenario 9.1: Two students are in a small disagreement and are not getting along with one another.
Scenario 9.2: Two students are arguing with one another.
Scenario 9.3: A student pushes and/or shoves another student.
Scenario 9.4: A student hits another student.
Scenario 9.5: A student is bullying and/or cyberbullying another student.
Scenario 9.6: Two students are physically fighting.
Scenario 9.7: A student hits the teacher.

We know these are not the only student conflict behaviors that happen in your classroom. These specific scenarios are a starting point for you to develop your Great Teacher Language (GTL) for your classroom. For some of our student behavior scenarios, we have included GTL examples for you to use when talking with parents. These GTL examples are templates for phone conversations, emails, or other types of messages to develop strong communication between teachers and parents and to promote understanding, relationships, trust, and collaboration.

With the many different needs, backgrounds, personalities, quirks, and idiosyncrasies among your students, conflicts are going to happen. Student conflicts range from small disagreements to bullying behaviors to actual physical fighting. Unless we take steps to prevent, defuse, and resolve student conflicts, they are bound to erupt into behaviors that are more frequent and intense. Your Language of Practice (LoP) in the form of GTL can offer these students in conflict the accountability, encouragement, grace, guidance, high expectations, hope, love, relationships, respect, understanding, and unity they need to help them work through their initial differences to prevent greater conflicts from occurring. This GTL can promote patience, love, grace, agreement, cooperation, teamwork, and the power of forgiveness to ensure unity in the classroom.

At any given moment, a conflict can occur in the classroom and teachers need a plan to prevent conflicts from happening, defuse conflicts in the moment, and promote unity by guiding students through the reconciliation process. This GTL plan begins by actively pursuing an in-depth understanding of student behaviors that lead to conflict. The following list illustrates a host of reasons that lead to student conflict in the classroom:

- Anger
- Bullying
- Competitiveness
- Disappointment
- Embarrassment
- Feeling disrespected
- Feeling insulted
- Feeling offended
- Fighting for possessions
- Greed
- Jealousy
- Misplaced anger
- Misplaced revenge
- Rejection
- Seeking power
- Seeking superiority

- Feeling sick
- Feeling wounded
- Selfishness
- Wanting revenge

When teachers begin to understand the many reasons for student conflict in their classroom, they are better able to help their students learn to avoid conflict with others. Showing students a better way to react before a conflict occurs and recognizing students who make positive choices to avoid conflicts are concrete steps in preventing student conflicts. Teachers need to provide opportunities for students to openly discuss the reasons for conflict and then role-play with students how to avoid conflicts before they happen. (At the end of this chapter, see GTL Classroom Activity entitled "Role-Play GTL Scenario for Students to Practice How to Avoid Conflicts Before They Happen.")

Many of the student conflicts in schools today begin with students who are angry and act out their aggression on others. Sometimes, students with angry and aggressive behaviors create a wall between themselves and the outside world. When others try to find a way in which to help, they are met with "Don't mess with me." Often students who display these angry and aggressive behaviors do not see the consequences of their own behaviors and how those behaviors affect others.

How do we intentionally break the cycle of student anger and aggression? Teachers need to offer these students concrete and effective strategies for dealing with their anger and aggression. Teachers need to work carefully and persistently with these students, paying special attention to each student's needs. For example, if the student demonstrates a pattern of anger and aggression, then the teacher can refer the student to a guidance counselor or school social worker. These students need to know that they "belong" and that they have a team of support rallying around them. They need to know that others are concerned about them and want to help them. Once these students begin to learn how to deal with their anger, they can begin to break the cycle of anger and aggression.

Tragically, a significantly large number of student conflicts in schools today are related to bullying and/or cyberbullying behaviors. Teachers need to recognize the short-term and lasting impact that bullying and cyberbullying can have on their students. Students who are being bullied may feel threatened and fearful at school. Their ability to focus on their learning is disrupted by the words and actions of a bully.

How do we intentionally break the cycle of bullying and cyberbullying that leads to students in conflict? What are you going to say to a bully? How will you address the needs of the student being bullied—and the bully? Both the person being bullied and the bully need your words of grace, hope, love, and accountability.

The bully must be held accountable. Students need to know that bullying is not acceptable—ever. It's not acceptable in the classroom. It's not acceptable on any digital device. They need to see the impact of "acting out" or "typing out" their aggression, the hurt it causes others, and accept the consequences for their behavior. They also need clear alternatives for working through their aggressive feelings and strategies for restoring relationships. A teacher's quick, kind, consistent, and firm response to bullying and cyberbullying behaviors can offer a way to end the cycle of bullying in the classroom and beyond.

The student being bullied needs your support and guidance as well. Your words and actions can offer them the confidence and encouragement to overcome their feelings of fear and revenge. When the student being bullied sees your quick, kind, consistent, and firm response to eliminating bullying behavior, that student—and everyone in the classroom—sees that bullying is unacceptable and the classroom becomes a safer place for learning.

Even with the best of prevention plans, there will be conflicts that escalate into major classroom disruptions with intense emotions and physical fighting. When these major disruptions occur, teachers need to immediately intervene with a plan to defuse the situation. Defusing a student conflict is more effective when the teacher has provided and discussed clear expectations for behavior and the consequences for fighting and bullying. (At the end of this chapter, see GTL Classroom Activity entitled "Revisiting the Classroom Rules and Clear Expectations for Behavior and the Consequences for Fighting and Bullying Behaviors."). The teacher's response needs to be calm, caring, impartial, and poised. Our language and actions need to convey to students that "I'm concerned for each of you. I really want to know what's going on here, but we all need to take a step back and cool down. Then we'll come together to discuss the problem."

When students are experiencing intense emotions from a physical conflict, they need time to cool down and regain their composure. By separating students and giving them time to cool down, we increase the likelihood of a rational and honest discussion at a later time. Once the cool-down period is over, students need to know that the teacher's ultimate goal is to understand the reason for the physical conflict and help students work through it. Therefore, teachers need to listen to both sides of the situation and respect the feelings and opinions of everyone involved.

Whether they know it or not, students in conflict have four specific needs:

1. The need to be heard. All students need to know they will be given the opportunity to share their side of the story without interruption and with a sincere attempt to listen for understanding.
2. The need to hear the other person's side of the story. When we challenge students to listen to each other and put themselves in the other person's situation, they learn a valuable life lesson regarding empathy and understanding.
3. The need for the truth to rise to the top. Getting to the truth can be difficult. The feelings and emotions surrounding conflict can cloud judgment and create confusion. Sometimes, students have forgotten the original reason for their disagreement. Often, other students are stirring the conflict. To get to the truth, teachers need to insist on honesty and encourage students to reflect on the past events that led to their conflict—what really happened.
4. The need for reconciliation. Students in conflict need to experience reconciliation with one another. What better life lesson can a student learn in your classroom than the one that teaches them that they can move from frustration to friendship, anger to understanding, and conflict to unity?

Conflict will not resolve itself, however, and students need a teacher's guidance to move toward reconciliation. When students experience the opportunity to resolve their conflict with unity as the goal, it takes the focus off themselves, and they begin to see their responsibility to the larger classroom community. They are more likely to value and appreciate others and experience the benefits of working, learning, and living in a unified classroom.

WHAT DO GREAT TEACHERS SAY WHEN...?

Two Students are in a Small Disagreement and Are Not Getting Along With One Another. (Scenario 9.1)

GTL Reminders to Self:

Remember... Provide clear examples and strategies for students to follow when they feel that a problem or disagreement is starting.

Words of Guidance

Remember... Let your students know that you care about them and that you will treat them all the same way.

Words of Accountability

Remember... If a student doesn't want to share what's wrong, don't force the issue. Be ready to listen when they are ready to talk.

Words of Understanding

Remember... By proactively surveying the classroom landscape to determine the relationship needs of your students and nurturing the growth of friendly relationships among your students, you can possibly help prevent small student disagreements.

Words of Understanding

GTL to Share with Students:

"To maintain classroom unity, it's important that we talk through our arguments with respect and understanding."

Words of Grace

"If you have a problem or disagreement with someone, you need to respectfully talk with that person to understand their side of the story. Listening and understanding how they feel can help you get along with each other."

Words of Guidance

"When you have a small disagreement with another student, be careful not to listen to the disrespectful or untrue things that other students might be saying about it. Instead, listen to students whom you trust and who are encouraging you to talk to the other student to work it out."

Words of High Expectations

"When you say those things to (that other student), it shows disrespect for him/her. What could you have said instead?"

Words of Respect

(Shared with the whole class) "I want all of us to work through our differences so we can work together, learn together, and grow together."

Words of Unity

(Shared with the whole class) "The classroom rules and behavior expectations we agreed on at the beginning of the year help us get along better with each other."

Words of Guidance

(Shared with the whole class) "When you have a problem with another student in our classroom, I'm going to ask you both to figure out a solution together."

Words of Accountability

(To the two students in a disagreement) "I noticed the two of you have not come to an agreement yet. I want to talk with you both about the situation, so we can figure out a solution together."

Words of Relationship

(To share with the whole class) "I care about all of you, so I'm going to hold each of you accountable for the choices you make."

Words of Love

WHAT DO GREAT TEACHERS SAY WHEN...?

Two Students Are Arguing With One Another. (Scenario 9.2)

GTL Reminders to Self:

Remember... There is a reason why kids act the way they do, so try to find out what's going on and what is driving those behaviors.

Words of Understanding

Remember... Be careful not to make assumptions about students and their circumstances. Instead, develop meaningful relationships with them that encourage success.

Words of Relationship

Remember... When students are emotionally charged, you can sometimes defuse the situation by asking the students to help you with something and then thanking them for their help.

Words of Guidance

Remember... Survey the classroom landscape and look for signs of student disagreements and be ready to offer strategies to avoid verbal arguments.

Words of Hope

GTL to Share with Students:

"There might be times when you get so angry with another student that you want to yell at them. But rather than doing that, take a step back, breathe, and take a minute to consider forgiving them."

Words of Grace

"When others are arguing with you and accusing you of something you haven't done, don't lash out and get defensive; instead, respectfully explain yourself and explain why you would not do that."

Words of Guidance

"I thought you were going to react differently in your group work today. I was glad to see that you made the choice to complete your work instead of getting into an argument with those other students. I'm proud of you."

Words of Encouragement

"Yesterday, I saw you talking to (the other student) about the issue between the two of you. We've been discussing ways to work through conflicts together in our class. When I saw you making the effort to get along, I was proud of you."

Words of Encouragement

"You both obviously have strong feelings about this issue. I'm hoping that the two of you can work it out together now, but if that's not possible, then the three of us will need to discuss these feelings and work together to resolve this problem."

Words of Guidance

"I can't allow this loud arguing in our classroom. You can cool down here, talk with me calmly in the hallway, or we can go and talk with the assistant principal or the guidance counselor. Which would you rather do? It's your choice."

Words of Accountability

"I have seen you handle this type of situation before. I know you can do it again. Let's talk about how you can make this right with (the other student)."

Words of Hope

"Help me understand why you're so angry with (another student). We need to get to the bottom of this issue so we can focus on our lesson. I'm wondering if it's a complete misunderstanding."

Words of Understanding

"You've been working so hard to get along with everyone. I'm going to call your parents and tell them what a great job you're doing of building friendships and getting along with students in our class."

Words of Encouragement

GTL to Use When Talking and Communicating with Parents:

Phone call to discuss a student's behavior in the classroom: A student is arguing with other students and disrupting class multiple times during the day.

(Note: This GTL phone conversation provides a template you can modify and send to parents as a letter, email, text message, etc.).

"Hello! My name is …. I'm Jamie's teacher. Is now a good time for us to talk?"

Words of Respect

"I enjoy having Jamie in my class. He is… (share something personal, positive, and specific that you've experienced with Jamie)."

Words of Encouragement

"At the beginning of the school year at the parent Open House, you and I talked about the importance of maintaining a strong relationship and open communication between home and school. That's why I called to share something that happened several times in class today. Throughout the day, Jamie was arguing with different students and disrupting our class and the learning."

Words of Accountability

"I talked with Jamie to get an understanding about his behavior. I asked Jamie to help me understand why he was arguing so much today. I asked him if he was frustrated or angry or didn't feel well. I also asked him if there's anything another student has done to cause him to argue this way."

Words of Understanding

"I want to get to the root of Jamie's arguing and for him to know that I'm not upset with him; however, his behavior was not acceptable—we can't accept this in our classroom."

Words of Understanding

"So, I wanted to reach out and make you aware of his behavior and work together to get to the bottom of what is going on with Jamie. Has Jamie shared anything with you about our class, or other students in our class, that could give us a better understanding of how he's feeling about school?"

Words of Understanding

"If you can think of anything we can do to make things better for Jamie, please let me know. My hope is for all of our students to feel safe, enjoy school, and learn every day."

Words of Hope

WHAT DO GREAT TEACHERS SAY WHEN...?

A Student Pushes And/Or Shoves Another Student. (Scenario 9.3)

GTL Reminders to Self:

Remember... If the circumstances around students pushing and shoving are unclear, get as close to the truth of the matter, discuss the inappropriateness of the behavior, then offer both students the opportunity to talk it through together and defuse the situation rather than have it escalate.

Words of Unity

Remember... Offer students a listening ear whenever they come to you to discuss a problem they are having with another student.

Words of Relationship

Remember... Some students may need to talk with you to discuss a problem they are having with another student.

Words of Relationship

Remember... Be aware of the situations throughout the school day that lend themselves to pushing and shoving (e.g., lining up to go to PE and lunch, walking down the hallways, or coming in from recess to get water).

Words of Guidance

Remember... When lining up for activities, students need to be reminded of the proper behavior expectations and the consequences for pushing and shoving others.

Words of Accountability

Remember... Sometimes, students act out anger and push other students because of physical problems or they don't feel good. They might need to talk to you or see the school nurse.

Words of Understanding

GTL to Share with Students:

"If you need somebody to talk to or you've got a problem that you think might cause you to act out in class, then come pull me to the side one-on-one before we get class started."

Words of Guidance

"Because I care about both of you, I am going to hold you both accountable for pushing and shoving each other. We need to talk together about what happened, how the pushing and shoving started, and we'll also talk about how to make sure this doesn't happen again."

Words of Love

"I really want to understand what's going on and what caused you to push that other student. I want to help you make it right with the other student and keep it from happening again."

Words of Relationship

"You are obviously too angry to talk about it right now, but once you cool down, we can get to the bottom of the pushing and shoving and eliminate it."

Words of Hope

"Let's start at the beginning—what made you so angry that you would push another student?"

Words of Understanding

"Remember it's important to respect each other as we line up. It doesn't matter if you're first or last in line, everybody will get a chance to go to (lunch, PE, the playground) and we're all going to get there at the same time."

Words of Respect

"In our classroom, we are going to treat others the way we want to be treated."

Words of High Expectations

WHAT DO GREAT TEACHERS SAY WHEN...?

A Student Hits Another Student. (Scenario 9.4)

GTL Reminders to Self:

Remember... Harsh words of accountability for students who hit another student can lead to students who are angry or withdrawn, and as a result, they focus more on the teacher's disrespect for them than on their own misbehavior.

Words of Accountability

Remember... Respectfully helping students realize and accept the consequences for their misbehavior can nurture the growth of personal accountability and self-management.

Words of Accountability

Remember... Having a culture of clear and high expectations for student behavior can help prevent misbehaviors before they happen. It allows students "in the moment" to consider the choice to meet those expectations.

Words of High Expectations

Remember... Before misbehaviors happen, it's important for you to make all students in your classroom

aware of the consequences for misbehaviors, especially the consequences if they hit another student.
Words of High Expectations

Remember... Rather than harboring ill feelings for a student who has hit another student in your classroom, demonstrate grace and dig deep to get at the root of the problem.
Words of Grace

Remember... When dealing with a student who has hit another student, step back, breathe, and speak calmly with the student.
Words of Respect

Remember... When students reach a point in time when they are capable of 'taking a step back' and recognizing their behavior is destructive for themselves and others, they are demonstrating characteristics of self-management.
Words of Hope

GTL to Share with Students:

"Can you help me understand what's wrong? This isn't like you. Do you want to talk about it?"
Words of Relationship

"Because you hit another student, we have to discuss your behavior and the consequences with the principal and your parents. We have school policies to make sure our school is a safe place for everyone, and the school's policy is clear about the consequences for hitting another student."
Words of Accountability

"When you are feeling angry, stop, count to 10, and think about the consequences before you react."
Words of Guidance

"Let's talk together so you can tell me what happened between you and (the other student)."
Words of Understanding

"I care about both of you, and I want to help you both work this out. So, how can the three of us work this out so it won't happen anymore?"
Words of Unity

"I'm glad we worked together on this plan for improving your behavior. I know it's going to work because you are a very determined person, and when you give your attention to something, you get it done!"
Words of Encouragement

GTL to Use When Talking and Communicating with Parents:

Phone call to discuss a student's behavior in the classroom: A student hits another student in your class.

(This phone call is coming from the principal's office. The principal and the teacher agree that the teacher will lead the phone conversation.)

"Hello! My name is …. I'm Jamie's teacher. Is now a good time for us to talk?"
Words of Respect

"At the beginning of the school year at the parent Open House, you and I talked about the importance of maintaining a strong relationship and open communication between home and school. That's why I'm calling to share something that happened in class today. Jamie hit another student in our class. The first thing I did was to speak to both students to get an understanding of what happened."
Words of Accountability

"Then I talked with Jamie individually to get an understanding of his behavior. I asked Jamie to help me understand why he hit the other student. I asked him if he was frustrated or angry or didn't feel well. I also asked Jamie if there was anything the other student did to cause him to hit the other student."

Words of Understanding

"I have Jamie here in the principal's office with me. He's going to tell you what happened."

Words of Accountability

(Jamie tells his parents what happened and is truthful.)

"We have school policies to make sure our school is a safe place for everyone, and the school's policy is clear about the consequences for hitting another student. (State your school's policy for this type of behavior.)"

Words of Accountability

"I want to get to the root of Jamie's behavior and for him to know that I'm not upset with him; however, his behavior was not acceptable—we can't accept this in our classroom."

Words of Understanding

"So, I wanted to reach out and make you aware of his behavior and work together to get to the bottom of what is going on with Jamie. Has Jamie shared anything with you about our class, or other students in our class, that could give us a better understanding of how he's feeling about school?"

Words of Understanding

"Before we finish our conversation, I wanted to share that I have enjoyed having Jamie in my class. He is… (share something personal, positive, and specific that you've experienced with Jamie)."

Words of Encouragement

"If you can think of anything we can do to make things better for Jamie, please let me know. My hope is for all of our students to feel safe, enjoy school, and learn every day."

Words of Hope

GTL to Use When Talking and Communicating with Parents:

Phone call to the parent of a student who was hit by another student in class.

(The student who has been hit wants to call their parents to let them know they are OK and to share what happened.)

"Hello! My name is …. I'm Mark's teacher. He's not in trouble. Is now a good time for us to talk?"

Words of Respect

"I'm calling you to share something that happened in class today. Another student in our class hit Mark. He's here with me and he wants to talk with you about what happened."

Words of Understanding

(Mark tells his parents what happened and is truthful.)

"The first thing I did was to speak to both students to get an understanding of what happened."

Words of Accountability

"Then I talked with Mark individually to get an understanding of how he's feeling about it. I asked him if he was hurt, needed to go to the nurse, or call home. He wanted to talk with you about it."

Words of Understanding

"We have school policies to make sure our school is a safe place for everyone, and the school's policy is clear about the consequences for hitting another student."

Words of Accountability

"Before we finish our conversation, I wanted to share that I have enjoyed having Mark in my class. He is... (share something personal, positive, and specific that you've experienced with Mark)."

Words of Encouragement

"If you can think of anything we can do to make things better for Mark, please let me know. My hope is for all of our students to feel safe, enjoy school, and learn every day."

Words of Hope

WHAT DO GREAT TEACHERS SAY WHEN...?

A Student is Bullying And/Or Cyberbullying Another Student. (Scenario 9.5)

GTL Reminders to Self:

Remember... Rather than harboring ill feelings for the students who are bullying other students, separate the student from the bullying behaviors, demonstrate grace to them, and dig deep to get to the root of the problem.

Words of Grace

Remember... When you are working with a student who is demonstrating bullying behaviors, address the bullying behaviors, but don't label the student as a bully.

Words of Love

Remember... Sometimes, you—alone—cannot solve a student's problem, and you will need the help of the guidance counselor and other support personnel.

Words of Guidance

Remember... Wanting to get to the root of the problem when dealing with student bullying is a sign of care and love.

Words of Love

Remember... No one likes to feel threatened. The student being bullied needs your attention and support.

Words of Relationship

Remember... Students who bully others may have been bullied themselves.

Words of Understanding

Remember... Be on the lookout and listening for potential bullying behavior. Sometimes, students who are being bullied start to withdraw and get silent. Your whole class can feel unsafe and negatively impacted by bullying behavior.

Words of Guidance

Remember... Be on the lookout and listening for potential cyberbullying behavior. Sometimes, students who are being cyberbullied start to withdraw and get silent. Your whole class can feel unsafe and negatively impacted by cyberbullying behavior.

Words of Guidance

GTL to Share with Students:

(Shared with the whole class) "I want this to be very clear to everyone. Our classroom is going to be a safe place, and bullying will not be tolerated."

Words of Accountability

(Shared with the whole class) "If another student is bullying you, here's what you need to do to stay safe and confident in our classroom. First, ask them respectfully to stop. If they refuse to stop, then you come to me, and we'll work through the problem and eliminate it."

Words of Guidance

"If you're being bullied, be sure not to keep your angry or scared feelings inside without sharing them with me or another adult. It's important to let someone know how you are feeling so they can help you with the problem."
Words of Guidance

"Be careful when you start to compare yourself to others. It could lead to feelings of insecurity and jealousy, which could lead to bullying behavior and conflicts."
Words of Guidance

(Private conversation with two students about bullying and cyberbullying behaviors) "Here's how we're going to discuss what's been happening at school and on your devices. Each of you will share your side of the story—and I expect both of you to be honest. I also expect each of you to listen respectfully to what the other person is saying and try to put yourself in the other person's place."
Words of Understanding

(Shared with the whole class) "We are going to work together to keep bullying from happening in our classroom. Let's treat others the way you want to be treated, so we can make our classroom safe and fun for everyone."
Words of High Expectations

(Shared with the whole class) "It is so important for all of us to understand how our words and actions can make others feel sad or angry. Let's remember to stop and think carefully about what we say and what we do to others in our classroom."
Words of Understanding

(Private conversation with a student) "You seem upset—what's going on? Is someone bothering you?"
Words of Love

"One of your classmates told me they feel like you are bullying them. Let's talk about it. I want to listen to you and try to understand what's going on."
                              Words of Understanding

GTL to Use When Talking and Communicating with Parents:

Phone call to discuss a student's behavior in the classroom: A student is bullying another student in your class.

(This phone call is coming from the principal's office. The principal and the teacher agree that the teacher will lead the phone conversation.)

"Hello! My name is …. I'm Jamie's teacher. Is now a good time for us to talk?"
                              Words of Respect

"I have Jamie here in the principal's office with me. He's going to tell you what happened today."
                              Words of Accountability

(Jamie tells his parents what happened and is truthful.)

"I want to get to the root of Jamie's behavior and for him to know that I'm not upset with him; however, his behavior was not acceptable—we can't accept this in our classroom."
                              Words of Understanding

"The first thing I did was to speak to both students to get an understanding of what happened."
                              Words of Accountability

"Then I talked with Jamie individually to get an understanding of his behavior. I asked Jamie to help me understand why he was bullying the other student. I asked him if he was frustrated or angry or didn't feel well. I also asked Jamie if there was anything the other student did to cause him to treat the other student that way."

Words of Understanding

"We have school policies to make sure our school is a safe place for everyone, and the school's policy is clear about the consequences for bullying another student. (State your school's policy for this type of behavior.)"

Words of Accountability

"I wanted to reach out and make you aware of his behavior and work together to get to the bottom of what is going on with Jamie. Has Jamie shared anything with you about our class, or other students in our class, that could give us a better understanding of how he's feeling about school?"

Words of Understanding

"Before we finish our conversation, I wanted to share that I have enjoyed having Jamie in my class. He is… (share something personal, positive, and specific that you've experienced with Jamie)."

Words of Encouragement

"If you can think of anything we can do to make things better for Jamie, please let me know. My hope is for all of our students to feel safe, enjoy school, and learn every day."

Words of Hope

GTL to Use When Talking and Communicating with Parents:

Phone call to the parent of a student who has been bullied by another student in class.

(The student who has been bullied wants to call their parents to let them know they are OK and to share what happened.)

"Hello! My name is …. I'm Mark's teacher. He's not in trouble. Is now a good time for us to talk?"
Words of Respect

"I'm calling you to share something that happened in class today. Another student admitted to bullying Mark in class. The first thing I did was to speak to both students to get an understanding of what happened. Mark's here with me and he wants to talk with you about it."
Words of Understanding

(Mark tells his parents what happened and is truthful.)

"After I talked with both students about what happened, I spoke with Mark individually to get an understanding of what happened to him. I also reassured Mark that bullying behaviors are unacceptable, and we want to make sure he feels cared for and safe at school."
Words of Understanding

"We have school policies to make sure our school is a safe place for everyone, and the school's policy is clear about the consequences for bullying another student."
Words of Accountability

"Before we finish our conversation, I wanted to share that I have enjoyed having Mark in my class. He is… (share something personal, positive, and specific that you've experienced with Mark)."
Words of Encouragement

"If you can think of anything we can do to make things better for Mark, please let me know. My hope is for all of our students to feel safe, enjoy school, and learn every day."
Words of Hope

WHAT DO GREAT TEACHERS SAY WHEN...?

Two Students Are Physically Fighting. (Scenario 9.6)

(This scenario is a serious one. Anytime students fight in your classroom, it is a chaotic, scary, and emotionally and physically charged experience for the two students, you, and all the students in the classroom. To help you handle the situation, engage your school principal and resource officers immediately when student fighting happens in your classroom. Hopefully, these GTL examples offer guidance and understanding for you during this very stressful experience.)

GTL Reminders to Self:

Remember... Keeping a close watch on possible personal conflicts that might happen between students and redirecting those students in a more positive direction may help prevent the outburst of a physical fight between them.

Words of Guidance

Remember... It's important for you to make all students aware of the consequences for fighting in your classroom. Knowing and understanding the consequences may deter students from making the choice to physically fight with another student.

Words of Accountability

Remember... Provide students a list of effective strategies they can use to prevent fighting before it happens (e.g., go to the teacher immediately when you have a conflict with another student, remove yourself from the situation, maintain respect for other students, or talk with the guidance counselor).

Words of Guidance

Remember... When a physical fight breaks out in your classroom, remain calm and get help from the principal and assistant principal immediately.

Words of Guidance

Remember... When a physical fight breaks out in your classroom, reassure the other students that you're going to take care of the situation and remind them they need to stay calm and move away from the fight.
Words of Guidance

Remember... When students are experiencing intense emotions from a physical conflict, they need time to cool down and regain their composure.
Words of Grace

Remember... Whether they know it or not, students in conflict have four specific needs: the need to be heard, the need to hear the other person's side of the story, the need for the truth to rise to the top, and the need for reconciliation.
Words of Love

Remember... Sometimes, students act out their anger on others because others have acted out their anger on them.
Words of Understanding

GTL to Share with Students:

"That's unacceptable classroom behavior, so you both need to separate, calm down, and regain your composure before we talk about what happened."
Words of Accountability

"Obviously, there is a problem here. I want to hear both sides of this problem, but first we need to step away and cool off."
Words of Accountability

"I'm not going to choose sides. Once you've cooled down, we'll have an honest discussion of what happened."
Words of Relationship

"I'm concerned for each of you. I really want to know what's going on here, but we all need to take a step back and cool down. Then we'll come together to discuss the problem."

Words of Unity

"What were you doing when the disagreement started, (Student 1)? What were you doing, (Student 2)? What could you have done differently to keep this from happening?"

Words of Accountability

"Let's talk about what just happened. We need to get the truth of what really happened and then decide what we could have said or done to prevent this fight."

Words of Accountability

"Because you were both fighting, we have to discuss your behavior and the consequences with the principal and your parents. We have school policies to make sure our school is a safe place for everyone, and the school's policy is clear about the consequences of fighting."

Words of Accountability

"Now that we have cooled down, what can we do to keep this from happening again?"

Words of Understanding

"Because of your behavior, you're going to be… (State your school's policy for fighting. If your school's policy is an out-of-school suspension, you can say…) We're going to send home your schoolwork, and you'll keep up with your assignments. We're going to call your parents right now and let you explain to them what happened and what you did."

Words of Accountability

(After the phone call with parents) "I appreciate your being honest with your parents about what happened—that's the first step in getting to the truth of what caused you to act that way. Once we know what caused it, we can learn how to prevent it from happening again."

Words of Encouragement

(Student returns to school after an out-of-school suspension for physical fighting) "I'm glad that you are back—we missed you. I'm looking forward to moving ahead and helping you in any way I can."

Words of Hope

GTL to Use When Talking and Communicating with Parents:

Phone call to discuss a student's behavior in the classroom: Two students have been physically fighting in your class.

(This phone call is coming from the principal's office. The principal and the teacher agree that the teacher will lead the phone conversation. The phone call is made to each student's parents individually).

"Hello! My name is … I'm Jamie's teacher. Is now a good time for us to talk?"

Words of Respect

"I'm calling to share something that happened in class today. Jamie got into a physical fight with another student in our class. I have Jamie here in the principal's office with me. He's going to tell you what happened."

(Jamie tells his parents what happened and is truthful.)

"I want you to know, the first thing I did was to speak to both students to get an understanding of what happened."

Words of Accountability

"Then I talked with Jamie individually to get an understanding of his behavior. I asked Jamie to help me understand what caused him to get into the fight with the other student. I asked him if he was frustrated or angry or didn't feel well. I also asked Jamie if there was anything the other student did to cause him to fight the other student."

                                                    Words of Understanding

"We have school policies to make sure our school is a safe place for everyone, and the school's policy is clear about the consequences for fighting with another student. Because of Jamie's behavior, he's going to be... (State your school's policy for fighting. If your school's policy is an out-of-school suspension, you can say ...) An out-of-school suspension doesn't mean he'll get behind in his schoolwork. We're going to send home his schoolwork, and he'll be able to keep up with his assignments."

                                                    Words of Accountability

"I want to get to the root of Jamie's behavior and for him to know that I'm not upset with him; however, his behavior was not acceptable—we can't accept this in our classroom."

                                                    Words of Understanding

"I wanted to reach out and make you aware of his behavior and work together to get to the bottom of what is going on with Jamie. Has Jamie shared anything with you about our class, or other students in our class, that could give us a better understanding of how he's feeling about school? If he shares more with you while he's home, please let me know. I really want to understand what caused this and how to keep it from happening again."

                                                    Words of Understanding

"Before we finish our conversation, I wanted to share that I have enjoyed having Jamie in my class. He is...

(share something personal, positive, and specific that you've experienced with Jamie)."

Words of Encouragement

"If you can think of anything we can do to make things better for Jamie, please let me know. My hope is for all of our students to feel safe, enjoy school, and learn every day."

Words of Hope

WHAT DO GREAT TEACHERS SAY WHEN...?

A Student Hits the Teacher. (Scenario 9.7)

(A student hits you! We're so sorry. This scenario is a personal one—and a serious one.

Anytime you get hit by a student—whether it's a slap on your arm unexpectedly or a more intense and aggressive act—it's physically and emotionally hurtful. Hopefully, these GTL examples offer encouragement and hope for you during this very stressful experience.)

GTL Reminders to Self:

Remember... In this type of situation, no one expects you to handle it perfectly. Protect yourself, protect the other students, and show yourself grace as you do the best you can.

Words of Love

Remember... The other students in the class are watching how you react and respond to this situation. Your actions and words in this very tough moment can defuse the situation with the aggressive student, model grace and self-control, and help the other students feel safe.

Words of Relationship

Remember… Do not retaliate when a student hits you. Protect yourself, stay poised, distance yourself from the student, and call for help immediately.

Words of Grace

Remember… When dealing with a student who has hit you, speak calmly with the student and reassure the other students that you're going to take care of the situation.

Words of Respect

Remember… Most of your days are spent working hard to understand your students and meet their needs. Unfortunately, your desire to understand your students is not always met with your students seeking to understand you and your needs. Be sure to spend time with your loved ones where your needs are valued and can be met.

Words of Understanding

Remember… Your loved ones are there for you when you experience the hardest days of being a teacher. They can offer you encouragement and support when you need it most.

Words of Relationship

Remember… Rather than harboring ill feelings for a student who has hit you, demonstrate grace and dig deep to get to the root of the problem and try to understand what triggered this student's anger and aggression.

Words of Grace

Remember… Rather than keeping your emotions about the incident to yourself, consider talking with a guidance counselor or an administrator at your school to discuss how you're feeling about the incident and how you're processing it.

Words of Hope

GTL to share with the aggressive student and the other students in the class, in the moment:

"Jamie, your behavior just now was against our school policy. I'm going to have to call the principal immediately."

Words of Accountability

"I don't have a choice here because of your behavior. We have to discuss this behavior with the principal and your parents."

Words of Accountability

(To the whole class) "Thank you for staying calm and for helping me with this situation. Please stay in your seats and work quietly while I call the principal."

Words of Guidance

(To the whole class) "Mrs. Jones (another teacher or assistant principal) is going to come and be with you while we go to the principal's office."

Words of Unity

GTL to share with the aggressive student in the principal's office:

"You know that I'll work with you to help you in any way I can, but hitting me was wrong. It hurt me. We can't hurt each other."

Words of Accountability

"Because of your behavior, you're going to be... (State your school's policy for hitting a teacher. If your school's policy is an out-of-school suspension, you can say ...) We're going to send home your schoolwork, and you'll keep up with your assignments. We're going to call your parents right now and let you explain to them what happened and what you did."

Words of Accountability

(After the phone call with parents) "I appreciate your being honest with your parents about what happened—that's the first step in getting to the truth of what caused you to act that way. Once we know what caused it, we can learn how to prevent it from happening again."

Words of Encouragement

(If the student apologizes to you) "I appreciate your apology, and I accept it and forgive you. I'll make sure you have the schoolwork you need to keep up with your assignments. I'm looking forward to your getting back to class."

Words of Grace

(If the student does not apologize to you) "I can see that you're still frustrated and need more time to cool down. I hope with more time, you'll come back to me to apologize. I'll make sure you have the schoolwork you need to keep up with your assignments. I'm looking forward to you getting back to class."

Words of Grace

GTL to Use When Talking and Communicating with Parents:

Phone call from the teacher to the parent to let the student explain what happened in class today when he hit the teacher.

(This phone call is coming from the principal's office. The principal and the teacher agree that the teacher will lead the phone conversation.)

"Hello! My name is …. I'm Jamie's teacher. Is now a good time for us to talk?"

Words of Respect

"I have Jamie here in the principal's office with me. He's going to tell you what happened."

Words of Accountability

(Jamie tells his parents what happened and is truthful.)

"Because of Jamie's behavior, he's going to be… (State your school's policy for hitting a teacher. If your school's policy is an out-of-school suspension, you can say …) An out-of-school suspension doesn't mean he'll get behind in his schoolwork. We're going to send home his schoolwork, and he'll be able to keep up with his assignments."
Words of Accountability

"This just happened a few minutes ago, so Jamie and I really haven't had a chance to talk about what caused this to happen, yet. If he shares more with you while he's home, please let me know. I really want to understand what caused this and how to keep it from happening again."
Words of Unity

"It's important for us to maintain a strong relationship and open communication between home and school."
Words of Relationship

"Before we finish our conversation, I wanted to share that I have enjoyed having Jamie in my class. He is… (share something personal, positive, and specific that you've experienced with Jamie)."
Words of Encouragement

"If you can think of anything we can do to make things better for Jamie, please let me know. My hope is that all of our students will feel safe, enjoy school, and learn as much as they can every day."
Words of Hope

GTL Classroom Activities to Transform Student Behavior and Your Classroom Culture

GTL Classroom Activities to Address Student Conflict in the Classroom

We see these activities as either "in the moment" or a time to circle up for classroom meetings to encourage student voice and student engagement in your classroom. We see the teacher as a facilitator and co-learner during these GTL activities and students as active participants in learning how to "see the classroom through the lens of the teacher" and how to manage their own behavior.

1. (Role-Play GTL Scenario for Students to Practice How to Avoid Conflicts Before They Happen.) Before the role-play, take a few minutes to openly discuss some reasons for conflict between students (anger, bullying, embarrassment, feeling insulted, fighting for possessions, greed, jealousy, selfishness, etc.). Select one student to role-play a teacher and two students to role-play students who are in a conflict. The conflict could be they are angry with each other because they each wanted to be first in line. Or you could use a different conflict to describe your specific classroom situation. Allow time for the two students who are in conflict to interact and argue with each other. Then allow time for the role-playing teacher to respond to the arguing students and give them strategies for avoiding the conflict. Encourage the other students in the class to help the role-playing teacher with what to say and to offer helpful strategies to avoid the conflict. Conclude the role-playing activity with a discussion of how you, as the teacher, would address the students to help avoid the conflict.
2. (Hit the Pause Button for Discussion on What Bullying Is and What To Do If You are Bullied.) Share with the students that you are going to "Hit the Pause Button" on the lesson and take important time to discuss what bullying is and what to do if you are bullied by someone.

Ask the students to share their thoughts on what bullying behaviors look like and sound like. Then together discuss what you can do if you are being bullied. List those strategies on the board. (For example: 1. Respectfully ask the other student to stop. 2. Walk away and stay away from the other student. 3. Don't bully them back. 4. Find an adult nearby. 5. Talk with your teacher. 6. Ask to talk with the guidance counselor, etc.). Conclude the discussion with suggestions and reminders of how the whole class can work together to prevent bullying: (1) Bullying and cyberbullying are not acceptable in our classroom—ever. (2) Treat others the way you want to be treated. (3) Understanding how others feel and putting the feelings of others before our own can make our classroom safe and fun for everyone.

3. (Revisiting the Classroom Rules and Clear Expectations for Behavior and the Consequences for Fighting and Bullying Behaviors) Remind the students about "Our Classroom Rules and Expectations" that everyone helped create and agreed to follow. Spend time discussing the classroom rules and expectations that apply to getting along with one another in our classroom. The expectations for the student list could include the following:
   1. I will respect the teacher and other students.
   2. I will not embarrass my classmates or my teacher.
   3. I will make good choices.
   4. I will work for win-win solutions with the teacher and other students, and so on.

   Also, discuss the school's discipline policy and the consequences for fighting and bullying. Explain the details of the policy and that bullying and cyberbullying are not acceptable—ever. Conclude the discussion by explaining that policies are in place to make sure school is safe and fun for everyone.

10

Transforming Your Classroom Culture into a Great Classroom Culture

Throughout this book, you've read hundreds of Great Teacher Language (GTL) examples to use with students and parents. Our hope is that you will adopt and integrate these GTL examples and make them your own. Your daily use of GTL with students and parents can transform your classroom culture into a Great Classroom Culture (GCC). A GCC is a culture built on the 11 GTL Word Categories. It's a culture of Accountability, Encouragement, Grace, Guidance, High Expectations, Hope, Love, Relationships, Respect, Understanding, and Unity. It's a strong and caring culture that will enhance learning! It's a culture that will transform student behavior and parent relationships! The GCC Framework (see Table 10.1) describes the transformational outcomes that students and parents can experience when a teacher promotes the 11 GTL Word Categories in their classroom!

This GCC starts with a teacher who uses GTL and models it for students. The students are impacted by GTL, and their behaviors are transformed. Parents are impacted by GTL, and they can experience the power of a positive and transformational relationship with you and the school.

TABLE 10.1 The Great Classroom Culture Framework

A Great Classroom Culture Promotes	So That Students	And Parents
Accountability	Reach personal accountability	Become well-informed supporters of their child and the teacher
Encouragement	Live a better way; become all they can be	Feel encouraged about their child and their child's school experiences
Grace	Experience and practice the power of forgiveness and second chances	See and hear the power of forgiveness and second chances for their child
Guidance	Practice self-management	Are confident their child is supported and will receive the personalized guidance and assistance they need throughout the year
High Expectations	Achieve their full potential	Will expect their child to achieve their full potential both in school and at home
Hope	Hope for and work for a better tomorrow	Experience ongoing hope for their child throughout the school year
Love	Experience and practice the selfless power and purpose of putting others first	Know without a doubt their child will experience unconditional care and receive loving accountability throughout the year
Relationships	Develop positive lifelong relationships with others	Experience the power of a positive and transformational relationship with you and the school
Respect	Model respect for self and others	Feel respected and valued by you
Understanding	Experience and practice empathy for others	Are heard, understood, and valued as vital partners in ensuring their child's success
Unity	Practice transformational teamwork through collaboration, agreement, and cooperation	Become personally engaged members of your classroom team

A GCC is a culture where teachers graciously offer encouragement, grace, guidance, high expectations, hope, love, and understanding to every student and to all parents. It's a culture where teachers work to develop relationships, share mutual respect, and promote unity with all students and their parents. It's a culture where teachers hold themselves and their students accountable to positive behavior expectations and are willing to share those behavior expectations with parents and ask for their support.

Once a teacher consistently uses and models GTL, student behavior transformation happens. For example, in a GCC, teachers encourage their students, so students encourage other students. Students experience grace from their teacher, so they show grace to other students. Teachers build relationships with students, so students build relationships with one another. Teachers provide students with respectful guidance toward positive behavior choices, and students learn how to become self-managed.

A GCC reflects a commitment to all the characteristics of the 11 GTL Word Categories. When teachers use and combine the 11 GTL Word Categories together into their Language of Practice, the results are transformational! For example, when Words of Love are combined with Words of Guidance and Words of Accountability, there's a tremendous transformational power that positively impacts students and parents!

The next section will provide descriptions of the 11 GTL Word Categories and powerful GTL Combinations that promote and support a GCC. Below, you'll notice the GTL Word Categories are italicized to highlight the power of these GTL combinations.

Powerful GTL Combinations that Promote a Great Classroom Culture

A GCC promotes *Accountability*. In a classroom culture that promotes *Accountability*, teachers and students are held *Accountable* for their words and actions <u>and</u> offered *Grace* <u>and</u> given the opportunity to get it right the next time. Teacher behavior expectations, student behavior expectations, and other positive behavior expectations are jointly determined on the first day of school and in the days that follow and are discussed frequently to *Guide* students toward making appropriate decisions about their behavior choices, which empowers students to practice personal accountability. To promote *Unity*, parents are included in the process as well by being asked to sign the student behavior expectations to indicate their agreement.

GTL Combinations for Students
When *Accountability* is combined with *Grace* and *Guidance*, teachers hold students *Accountable* all along the way, separate the student from the behavior, forgive their past mistakes, give them another chance to get it right, and help students find a path to success and appropriate behavior so that students reach personal *Accountability* and practice self-management.

GTL Combinations for Parents
When *Accountability* is combined with *Unity*, teachers provide parents a clear and *Respectful* account of their child's classroom behavior and create a transformational culture of collaboration and teamwork with all parents so that parents become personally engaged members of your classroom team.

A GCC promotes *Encouragement*. In a classroom culture that promotes *Encouragement*, teachers *Encourage* themselves (GTL Reminders to Self) and their students to be the best they can be both academically and in their behavior choices. Students are *Encouraged* and *Guided* to reach their potential, overcome their fears, and keep on trying. Teachers *Encourage* themselves and their students with the confidence to do the right thing for themselves and demonstrate *Love* and care for others. When teachers *Encourage* parents about their child and their child's school experiences, they positively inspire parents and build powerful *Relationships* with them.

GTL Combinations for Students

When *Encouragement* is combined with *Love*, teachers rally students with the courage to overcome challenges, obstacles, barriers, failures, defeats, fears, and apathy; touch students' hearts; and demonstrate love and care unconditionally so that students live a better way, become all they can be, and experience and practice the selfless power and purpose of putting others first.

GTL Combinations for Parents

When *Encouragement* is combined with building *Relationships*, teachers inspire parents with positive support and *Encouragement*. When parents feel *Encouraged* about their child and their child's school experience, a trusting, caring, *Respectful*, and positive connection is formed, and a transformational *Relationship* between the teacher, the parents, and the school is established.

A GCC promotes *Grace*. In a classroom culture that promotes *Grace*, teachers demonstrate *Understanding, Love*, patience, and *Respect* for all students despite what they choose to do, hold them *Accountable* for those choices, and then offer them *Grace* to get it right the next time. Teachers share unconditional *Love* and support for students despite what those students may choose to do. In a culture of *Grace*, teachers do not harbor ill feelings toward students; instead, teachers practice the act of forgiveness and *Guide* their students to practice the act of forgiveness toward others as well. *Grace* is demonstrated to parents when teachers offer their child another chance to get it right and forgive their child's past mistakes.

GTL Combinations for Students

When *Grace* is combined with *Understanding*, teachers separate the student from the behavior, forgive their past mistakes, give them another chance to get it right, and work to discover the student's perspective so that students experience and practice the power of forgiveness and second chances and experience and practice empathy for others.

GTL Combinations for Parents
When *Grace* is combined with *Guidance*, teachers show parents that they offer all students another chance to get it right and forgive their past mistakes. Teachers inform parents of the *Guidance* and assistance they and the school will provide to their child, so that parents see and hear the power of forgiveness and second chances for their child.

A GCC promotes *Guidance*. In a classroom culture that promotes *Guidance*, teachers are the *Guide* for their students both academically and behaviorally. As teachers *Guide* their students, they give them a positive and supportive path to appropriate behavior choices. Teachers offer their students advice to *Guide* them all along the way. They offer students specific advice: "Next time try this or do this"—"Consider doing this"—"Here's another way". As teachers *Respectfully Guide* their students, they offer them an opportunity to improve both academically and behaviorally. The end goal of a culture of *Guidance* is when students choose to be self-managed in their behavior choices and their learning. Teachers demonstrate *Guidance* when they inform parents of the *Guidance* and assistance they and the school will provide to their child.

GTL Combinations for Students
When *Guidance* is combined with *Respect*, teachers help students find a path to success and appropriate behavior and demonstrate a mutual admiration for one another so that students practice self-management and model *Respect* for self and others.

GTL Combinations for Parents
When *Guidance* is combined with *High Expectations*, teachers inform parents of the *Guidance* and assistance they and the school will provide to their child to help their child envision and pursue their best schoolwork and behavior. Parents are confident their child is supported and will receive the personalized *Guidance* and assistance they need throughout the year, and parents expect their child to achieve their full potential both in school and at home.

A GCC promotes *High Expectations*. In a classroom culture that promotes *High Expectations*, teachers set the bar high by expecting the best from all students and themselves. When teachers set *High Expectations* with *Guidance* for their students, they help their students to envision and pursue their best. Setting *High Expectations* and conveying the anticipation that all students will meet them create a culture that expects all students to achieve their full potential both academically and behaviorally. Sharing *High Expectations* with parents demonstrates how teachers will help their child envision and pursue their best schoolwork and behavior.

> **GTL Combinations for Students**
> When *High Expectations* are combined with *Guidance*, teachers help students envision and pursue their best and help students find a path to success and appropriate behavior so students achieve their full potential and practice self-management.
>
> **GTL Combinations for Parents**
> When *High Expectations* are combined with *Hope*, teachers demonstrate to parents how they will help their child envision and pursue their best schoolwork and behavior, which inspires parents to look beyond the current circumstances and expect greater things for their child, so parents experience ongoing *Hope* for their child throughout the school year.

A GCC promotes *Hope*. In a classroom culture that promotes *Hope*, both teachers and students are *Encouraged* to see themselves and others with great potential. Teachers and students dare to dream—dream of how they can actually achieve more than they expected. Students gain the confidence that what they *Hope* for—what they dream of—can happen! *Hope* can spark students' interests and inspire them to learn more than ever before and change their behavior choices. When teachers share *Hope* with parents, they inspire parents to look beyond the current circumstances and expect greater things for their child.

GTL Combinations for Students
When *Hope* is combined with *Encouragement*, teachers inspire a vision of a better tomorrow and rally students with the courage to overcome challenges, obstacles, barriers, failures, defeats, fears, and apathy so students *Hope* for and work for a better tomorrow, live a better way, and become all they can be.

GTL Combinations for Parents
When *Hope* is combined with *High Expectations*, teachers inspire parents to look beyond the current circumstances and expect greater things for their child. Teachers demonstrate to parents how they will help their child envision and pursue their best schoolwork and behavior, and then parents will expect their child to achieve their full potential both in school and at home.

A GCC promotes *Love*. This *Love* is never to be confused with a romantic love, nor should it be shared without *Accountability*. In a classroom culture that promotes *Love*, teachers demonstrate an unconditional *Love* and care for students. Students feel valued and supported while being held *Accountable* for the actions they choose. In a culture of *Love*, teachers demonstrate the patience to endure students' misbehavior choices, dig deep to *Understand* each student's needs, and make an unwavering commitment to the belief that all students can improve. As teachers demonstrate *Love* and care for students, they inspire their students to use their own words and actions to help other students and practice empathy for them and others. When teachers demonstrate *Love* and care for parents and their child, they touch parents' hearts and trusting *Relationships* begin to develop.

GTL Combinations for Students
When *Love* is combined with *Understanding*, teachers touch students' hearts and demonstrate *Love* and care unconditionally. They also seek to *Understand* the student's perspective, so students experience and practice the selfless power and purpose of putting others first and experience and practice empathy for others.

GTL Combinations for Parents
When *Love* is combined with *Relationships*, teachers touch parents' hearts and demonstrate *Love* and care for them and their child unconditionally. They also establish a trusting, caring, *Respectful*, and positive connection with every parent so parents experience the power of a positive and transformational *Relationship* with you and the school.

A GCC promotes building *Relationships*. In a classroom culture that promotes building *Relationships* with all students, teachers are committed to getting to know every one of their students personally. Teachers make a conscious effort to create meaningful connections with students by showing each student they are valued and worth their time and attention. Students trust their teacher when they feel emotionally safe and know that their teacher *Loves* and cares about them and wants the best for them. As teachers build *Relationships* with their students, they talk with students and spend time individually with them to discover their passions, talents, and interests. When teachers build *Relationships* with students, they demonstrate a desire to work with students to break down walls, build bridges, and reach common ground. When teachers build *Relationships* with parents, they establish a trusting, caring, *Respectful*, and positive connection with every parent.

GTL Combinations for Students
When *Relationships* are combined with *Love*, teachers establish a caring and positive connection with each student, touch their hearts, and demonstrate *Love* and care unconditionally so students develop positive lifelong *Relationships* with others and experience and practice the selfless power and purpose of putting others first.

GTL Combinations for Parents
When *Relationships* are combined with *Unity*, teachers establish a trusting, caring, *Respectful*, and positive connection with every parent and create a transformational culture

of collaboration and teamwork with all parents so parents experience the power of a positive and transformational *Relationship* with them and the school and become personally engaged members of your classroom team.

A GCC promotes *Respect*. In a classroom culture that promotes *Respect*, teachers demonstrate a careful consideration and appreciation for all students and themselves. When teachers make a deliberate attempt to *Understand* a student's perspective about a behavior or learning situation, they demonstrate *Respect* for students and their needs. As teachers model *Respect* for themselves and their students, it reveals a desire to value all students and demonstrates a proper regard for the dignity of their own character and the character of their students. As teachers use words of *Respect* with students, it builds a model for mutual *Respect* between the teacher and all students. When teachers use words of *Respect* with parents, it demonstrates an intentional consideration and appreciation for all parents, and parents feel *Respected* and valued.

GTL Combinations for Students
When *Respect* is combined with *Understanding*, teachers and students demonstrate a mutual admiration for one another, and teachers discover the student's perspective so students model *Respect* for self and others and experience and practice empathy for others.

GTL Combinations for Parents
When *Respect* is combined with *Guidance*, teachers demonstrate an intentional consideration and appreciation for all parents and inform parents of the *Guidance* and assistance they and the school will provide to their child. Parents feel *Respected* and valued and are confident their child is supported and will receive the personalized *Guidance* and assistance they need throughout the year.

A GCC promotes *Understanding*. In a classroom culture that promotes *Understanding*, teachers demonstrate a conscious and deliberate effort to *Understand* their students' perspective in all situations. When individual student behavior or learning issues arise, teachers intentionally attempt to put themselves in the student's position to see things and *Understand* things from their perspective. Teachers want to *Understand* what's going on with the student and ask thoughtful questions to get to the root of the problem. As teachers spend quality time with individual students attempting to *Understand* their perspective, *Relationships* of trust are built. In a culture of *Understanding*, the ultimate goal is for teachers and students to experience and practice empathy for others. When teachers seek to *Understand* the parents' perspective, parents feel heard, understood, and valued as vital partners in ensuring their child's success.

GTL Combinations for Students
When *Understanding* is combined with *Relationships*, teachers discover the student's perspective and establish a caring and positive connection with each student, so students experience and practice empathy for others and develop positive lifelong *Relationships* with others.

GTL Combinations for Parents
When *Understanding* is combined with *Accountability*, teachers demonstrate their desire to truly *Understand* the parents' perspective while providing parents a clear and *Respectful* account of their child's classroom behaviors, so parents are heard, *Understood*, and valued as vital partners in ensuring their child's success and become well-informed supporters of their child and the teacher.

A GCC promotes *Unity*. In a classroom culture that promotes *Unity*, teachers *Encourage* a sense of belonging by ensuring that all students know they are valued and their participation in classroom activities, including the development of the classroom behavior expectations, is vital to the team. On the first day of school, teachers and students collaborate to create the behavior expectations for each other. Throughout the year, the teacher and students work together to hold each other *Accountable* for these agreed-upon behavior expectations. In a culture of *Unity*, the goal is to transform a group of individuals into a team culture. This team culture promotes collaboration, agreement, and cooperation with your students. Teachers also promote *Unity* with parents by inviting and *Encouraging* them to be active team members of the classroom.

GTL Combinations for Students
When *Unity* is combined with *Accountability*, teachers nurture a culture of collaboration and teamwork in their classroom and hold students *Accountable* all along the way, so students practice transformational teamwork through collaboration, agreement, and cooperation and reach personal *Accountability*.

GTL Combinations for Parents
When *Unity* is combined with *Respect*, teachers create a transformational culture of collaboration and teamwork with all parents by demonstrating an intentional consideration and appreciation for all parents. Parents feel *Respected* and valued by the teacher and become personally engaged members of the classroom team.

Now that you have read this book, our hope is that you will be encouraged, excited, and ready to try GTL! We've seen amazing transformations happen when teachers use it and share it with students and parents. Student behavior is transformed, parent relationships are transformed, and your classroom culture is transformed. A GCC of collaboration, teamwork, and strong relationships among teachers, students, and their parents emerges when teachers use GTL. Other transformational changes can happen across your school community as well. GTL and a GCC can break the burnout-to-dropout cycle and prevent student burnout, parent burnout, and teacher burnout. Using GTL and creating a GCC promote vitality for you and your school community! The GTL and GCC Frameworks can revitalize and support the existing student behavior management plans in your school. Students, parents, and teachers experience a school culture with vitality where they feel respected, valued, and successful. Students, parents, teachers, and **you** get to experience school in a transformed way—where we all get to experience happiness, hope, and joy!

Index of GTL Student Behavior Scenarios

Chapter 4: What Do Great Teachers Say When a Student is Passively Disengaged?

Scenario 4.1: A student is texting on his cell phone or scrolling through his computer.
Scenario 4.2: A student is sleeping in class.
Scenario 4.3: A student is not working on his assignment and looks embarrassed, troubled, stressed and/or frustrated.
Scenario 4.4: A student is not paying attention to the lesson and is daydreaming in class.
Scenario 4.5: A student never verbally participates in class.
Scenario 4.6: A passively disengaged student has failing grades in your class.

Chapter 5: What Do Great Teachers Say When a Student is an Attention Seeker?

Scenario 5.1: A student is constantly raising his/her hand and saying, "Teacher, Teacher…"
Scenario 5.2: A student is up out of his/her seat, socializing with other students, throwing away trash, sharpening his/her pencil, etc.
Scenario 5.3: A student says, "Teacher, he's bothering me!"
Scenario 5.4: A student is being the class entertainer.
Scenario 5.5: A student is always raising his/her hand, wanting to answer every question or is constantly asking questions.
Scenario 5.6: A student is always talking in class.

Chapter 6: What Do Great Teachers Say When a Student Outburst Happens?

Scenario 6.1: A student yells out, "This is so boring!"
Scenario 6.2: A student yells out, "This is stupid. I can't do it!"

Scenario 6.3: A student yells out, "Why do we need to learn this?"

Scenario 6.4: A student yells out profanity, "@#$%"

Scenario 6.5: A student yells out a verbally aggressive outburst and/or acts out a physically aggressive outburst.

Chapter 7: What Do Great Teachers Say When a Student Does Not Show Respect for Themselves or Others?

Scenario 7.1: A student is calling other students names and/or making fun of other students.

Scenario 7.2: A student is making inappropriate gestures at other students and/or the teacher.

Scenario 7.3: A student is verbally disrespectful to the teacher.

Scenario 7.4: A student is interrupting another student and/or the teacher.

Scenario 7.5: A student is taking things that do not belong to him/her.

Scenario 7.6: A student is demonstrating a lack of self-respect.

Chapter 8: What Do Great Teachers Say When a Student Refuses to Cooperate or Challenges You?

Scenario 8.1: A student consistently asks questions that challenge you and/or the lesson you are teaching.

Scenario 8.2: A student says, "I don't agree with you" or "I don't believe you" or "You are wrong!"

Scenario 8.3: A student refuses to cooperate with you and says, "You're not my mom. You can't tell me what to do! You can't make me do this work!"

Scenario 8.4: A student is outwardly angry and blatantly disrespectful toward you.

Chapter 9: What Do Great Teachers Say When a Student Conflict Occurs?

Scenario 9.1: Two students are in a small disagreement and are not getting along with one another.

Scenario 9.2: Two students are arguing with one another.

Scenario 9.3: A student pushes and/or shoves another student.
Scenario 9.4: A student hits another student.
Scenario 9.5: A student is bullying and/or cyberbullying another student.
Scenario 9.6: Two students are physically fighting.
Scenario 9.7: A student hits the teacher.

For Product Safety Concerns and Information please contact our EU
representative GPSR@taylorandfrancis.com
Taylor & Francis Verlag GmbH, Kaufingerstraße 24, 80331 München, Germany

www.ingramcontent.com/pod-product-compliance
Lightning Source LLC
Chambersburg PA
CBHW050634300426
44112CB00012B/1796